Financial Ratios

How to use financial ratios
to maximise value and success
for your business

Richard Bull

AMSTERDAM • BOSTON • HEIDELBERG • LONDON
NEW YORK • OXFORD • PARIS • SAN DIEGO
SAN FRANCISCO • SINGAPORE • SYDNEY • TOKYO

CIMA Publishing is an imprint of Elsevier

ELSEVIER

CIMA
PUBLISHING

CIMA Publishing is an imprint of Elsevier
Linacre House, Jordan Hill, Oxford OX2 8DP, UK
30 Corporate Drive, Suite 400, Burlington, MA 01803, USA

First edition 2008

British Library Cataloguing in Publication Data
A catalogue record for this book is available from the British Library

978 0 7506 8453 8

For information on all CIMA publications
visit our website at books.elsevier.com

Typeset by Integra Software Services Pvt. Ltd, Pondicherry, India
www.integra-india.com

Printed and bound by CPI Group (UK) Ltd, Croydon, CR0 4YY
Transferred to Digital Print 2012

Contents

List of Figures and Tables   v

Foreword   vii

Acknowledgements   viii

About the Author   ix

Introduction: The place of financial ratios in business success   xi

PART ONE   The Role of Financial Ratios   1

1   Creating value – a model of success   3

2   Measuring value – the origin of financial ratios   17

PART TWO   Understanding Financial Ratios   33

3   Funding management – the gearing ratio   35

4   Asset management – the asset turnover ratio   45

5   Value add management – the profit margin   61

6   Tax management – the effective tax rate   77

7   Growth management – the payout and retention ratios   87

PART THREE   Using Financial Ratios   99

8   The composite ratios   101

9   The place of financial ratios in strategic management   115

10   Perspectives on financial ratios   131

Appendices   143

Appendix 1   The purpose of ratios: The
three Eff's   145

Appendix 2   The source and application of
financial data for ratio analysis   149

Appendix 3   A benchmarking example   157

Appendix 4   Further reading   163

Index   167

List of Figures and Tables

Figures

I.1	The three Eff's	xv
I.2	The components of a process	xvi
I.3	The Enterprise Stewardship Model	xvii
1.1	Strategic management	6
1.2	Funding management	7
1.3	Asset management	8
1.4	Value add management	11
1.5	Tax management	12
1.6	Growth management	14
2.1	Business as a process for measurement	20
2.2	The strategic ratios	21
2.3	The gearing ratio	22
2.4	The asset turnover ratio	23
2.5	The profit margin	24
2.6	The effective tax rate	25
2.7a	The retention ratio	26
2.7b	The payout ratio	26
2.8	The financial ratios	27
2.9	The composite ratios	28
3.1	Funding management	38
4.1	Asset management	47
4.2	Analysis of assets on the balance sheet	50
4.3	Classes of assets	57
5.1	Value add management	64
5.2	The relationship between profit and value added	65
5.3	Two approaches to cost management	67
5.4	Three approaches to profit management	68
5.5	Alternative ways of doubling your profit margin	70
5.6	The enterprise value chain	73
6.1	Tax management	81
7.1	Growth management	90
7.2	Techniques of investment appraisal	93
8.1	Benchmarking results and processes for your business	104
8.2	The return on assets ratio	107

8.3	The return on equity ratio	108
8.4	The dividend yield	109
8.5	The composite ratios	111
9.1	The strategic management ratio	118
9.2	Five steps in the strategic management process	119
9.3	Checking the foundations	125
9.4	Strategic building maintenance	126
10.1	The customer and supplier perspectives on the profit margin	136
10.2	The employee perspective on ROA	137
10.3	The community perspective on after-tax ROA	138
10.4	The shareholder and entrepreneur perspectives on yields	140
10.5	The leadership perspective on roles and relationships	141
A2.1	The source of financial data for ratio analysis	152
A2.2	The application of financial data for ratio analysis	152
A2.3	Worked example: A jewellery group	154
A2.4	Worked example: An international oil company	155
A3.1	Benchmarking example – selected company data	159
A3.2	Benchmark mapping	160

Tables

A1.1	The Three Eff's – Definitions	147
A1.2	The Three Eff's – Examples	148

Foreword

A key element in the difference between success and failure in business start-ups is the ability of entrepreneurs to come to grips with the financial aspects of the business. Relatively few companies are started by accountants, and the sorts of people who have entrepreneurial drive are unlikely to regard financial ratios as an absorbing subject.

Hence it is important that books on the subject should be eminently readable and present the necessary information in such a way as to give it a 'story line'.

This Richard Bull's book does extremely well, putting ratios in the context of the successive stages of building a business, from the original idea, through the formulation of strategy to the realisation of added value. He concludes by looking at financial ratios from the perspectives of the different stakeholders – the customers, the employees, the suppliers, the community and the shareholders.

The author does remind us, however, of the dangers inherent in measuring business success through financial ratios alone.

I would strongly recommend this work as essential reading, not only for budding entrepreneurs, but for all those from non-financial backgrounds whose career paths take them into jobs that carry profit responsibility. It will also be of value to business studies students as a 'crammer'.

Philip Sadler CBE
formerly Chief Executive of Ashridge Management College

Acknowledgements

Thank you to those who have contributed to this book. It represents a further step in realising a vision for revealing the essence of business and what it means to all those engaged in it. In particular, I would like to thank:

David Auger BSc FCA;

Neil Austin BSc FCA MSI, Partner at KPMG and Global Head of Markets;

Dr David Hillson FRSA FAPM FIRM FCMI, Director of Risk Doctor and Partners; and

Gordon B.F. McKay MIOM, Managing Director of GBFM Consulting Ltd

for their comments and amendments to the original draft. They have each contributed to its character and integrity.

My thanks too to Andrew Boyd for his help in producing the introductory video for the CD-ROM included with this book.

About the Author

Richard Bull graduated in Politics, Philosophy and Economics from Oxford University before qualifying as an accountant with the Chartered Institute of Management Accountants (CIMA). He draws from his experience in a number of financial management positions in manufacturing and financial services over twenty years, including management consultancy assignments across a variety of industries. He is also a member of the Institute of Business Consulting (IBC).

Richard has written for a number of professional journals on many aspects of financial management and performance measurement and received an award from the International Federation of Accountants for his 'distinct and valuable contribution to the advancement of management accounting'.

He can be contacted via the publishers or through e-mail at enterprise.s@btinternet.com

Introduction: The place of financial ratios in business success

The place of financial ratios in measuring value and success in business

'What gets measured gets managed.' This has become an established principle in business. But is what we measure always what we want to manage? And is the target for our measurement what we really want to achieve?

A ratio expresses the relationship between two things. Expressed arithmetically, it is one number (the 'numerator') divided by another (the 'denominator'): 1/2, 2/1, 5/8, expressed as 1:2, 2:1 or 5:8 respectively.

A ratio can also measure the performance of a process. It can measure the amount of output from a process divided by the amount of input to that process. In this way we may derive a measure of productivity, say 100 widgets per person or 100 kilowatts per hour and so on. This can help us test the result of management actions designed to improve the performance of a process – an essential component in the 'plan-do-check-act' (PDCA) decision loop so familiar to students of management.

Financial ratios seek to measure the performance of a process by using a common unit of measure – money. To be precise, the monetary value attributed to things. In this way they can conveniently eliminate the units of measure of widgets, energy or even people and reduce the ratio back to its numeric form: 1:2, 2:1, 5:8 and so on.

Where success can be measured in purely financial terms then financial ratios can be a convenient way of measuring, and managing, success. But if true success – even happiness – defies measurement in financial terms then, while financial ratios may provide helpful proxies, they should be used with caution. We should be quite clear where they do not express fully what we seek to achieve. Otherwise we may achieve the outcome they inevitably lead us to rather than the success we ultimately seek.

Key challenges

1. How do we measure value and success?
2. What can we measure using financial ratios in a business?
3. How can we best describe a generic process for a business or enterprise?

The purpose of this book

And so this book provides both a guide and a warning for people who wish to make a success of the business in which they are engaged. It provides a road map of the steps that any business has to follow – from start-up to maturity. It illustrates how financial ratios seek to measure the way those steps are performed. And it describes some of the ways in which you might use those ratios to maximize the value and success you seek to achieve in your business.

Financial Ratios therefore stands out from other books on the subject. Other authors go to great lengths to explain what each ratio is called, how to calculate it, and what its numeric value is for different companies or industries. Their books tend to start with a particular ratio and then explain what it does, with a lot of numbers along the way.

My approach is to start at the business end. I begin by setting out the key management processes in any business or enterprise, what a successful business requires of them, and how to use financial ratios to measure that success. You will not find many numbers in this book.

This book is not an instruction manual. It will not tell you what you must do in each case to maximize value and achieve success. The criteria for determining value differ in different markets and industries where risks and opportunities vary. And the standards set for judging success differ in different cultures, where requirements and priorities vary.

This might sound extremely unsettling in a world where success in business is so often judged by profitability, market value and dividend yield – the trappings of 'the bottom line'. However, such trappings have often proved to be exactly that: traps for the unwary – especially the investor who is easily taken in by 'headline' figures.

They have in turn proved to be too strong a temptation for the unprincipled accountants or 'financial engineers', who have found ways to manipulate the figures to deceive the unwary.

It is for just this reason that this book is required reading for those who seek to understand the substance behind the headlines. It is for those who want to both contribute to and share in the success of an enterprise – not just for today but in whatever time frame is appropriate for them.

If you are a shareholder or investor, broker or analyst, CEO or non-executive director, it is important that you are able to put the financial results of an enterprise in proper context, expressed in ratio form or otherwise. You will then be able to judge the relevance of the data you are presented with. And you will be able to ask the right questions about it so that you can convert such data into real information. It is only then that you will be in a position to make properly informed decisions.

Value and success in business

The terms 'business' and 'enterprise' are often used interchangeably. However, when examining financial ratios as tools of performance measurement there is a subtle distinction which may be helpful.

Where 'business' refers simply to a level of activity (or 'busyness'), the appropriate measurement of its performance would be the amount of resources employed in it and the degree to which they are utilised. Thus measures of speed, production and productivity would be most relevant. However 'enterprise' implies a sense of purpose. The appropriate measure of performance will then depend on what that purpose is. It is here that the concept of 'success' becomes relevant but at the same time difficult to generalise.

If the measure of success of a company is the amount of hard cash it is generating for the owners or shareholders, then the level of dividends being distributed to them would be the ultimate measure. As soon as one looks beyond today, one would want to look at how capable the company is of maintaining or increasing that distribution. Key measures would then include its profitability, return on equity and such things as dividend cover. Already we are adding to complexity and increasing the risk of confusion.

The levels of complexity increase substantially when we consider more subtle measures of success. The above only considers the interest of shareholders. In reality businesses incorporate a variety of other interests as well: employees, suppliers, customers, and providers of local services. This is the wider community of stakeholders. They are all critical to the success of an enterprise and, to the extent that 'value and success are in the eye of the beholder', they will each have their own perspective on the value of a business.

We fulfil many of these various roles ourselves – as customer, supplier, employee or interested member of the public – in the different enterprises that we are engaged with. Consideration of these wider, no less legitimate interests, calls for new criteria for judging success and new benchmarks for measuring value. A company's actions have effects on a wide variety of interests which in turn can affect its own success.

Finally, we consider the real purpose for which an enterprise was initiated. Here its success must be measured by the extent to which the original vision or idea for the enterprise has been realised. Visions can have tangible and intangible elements and may not even be capable of measurement when first conceived. This makes the task of assessing their achievement that much more challenging by using financial measures alone.

The 'Three Eff's'

When we seek to measure the value and success of an enterprise we can look at its performance in three different perspectives. Each dimension can be applied to the enterprise as a whole or to separate processes within it.

The first perspective is *efficiency*. Measures of efficiency take the inputs to a process and assess how economically they are used to produce a given output. They therefore tend to focus on *cost*. A second perspective is *effectiveness*. Measures of effectiveness assess the value of output produced from a given set of resources. This subtly shifts our focus from measuring inputs to measuring output. When using financial measures it represents a shift from measuring cost to measuring *value*. The final perspective is *efficacy*. This is a little-used term but one which describes this third dimension of performance very aptly. Measures of efficacy assess the degree to which the inputs produced the result intended and thereby contributed to the achievement of the true purpose of the enterprise. Here we venture into aspects of value which are often less tangible and have more to do with measuring *success*. It is therefore more difficult to apply financial measures as we progress through these perspectives.

These three perspectives are illustrated in Figure I.1. A company's vision is mapped against five criteria (A, B, C, D and E). Three different sets of performance results are then mapped over it to illustrate the three different perspectives: efficiency, effectiveness and efficacy.

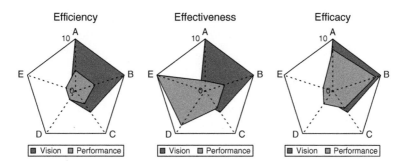

Figure I.1 The three Eff's

In the first case the enterprise might be seen to be achieving success through its efficiency. The vision is being mirrored by performance, but constrained in every direction by an over-emphasis on efficiency. In the second case some criteria are being achieved effectively but at the expense of others, and the vision has been distorted in the process. The third case illustrates efficacy. Performance reflects the shape of the vision and is largely fulfilling it.

Financial ratios are of themselves *quantitative* in nature. They are therefore most appropriate as measures of efficiency. The more we understand the processes that lie behind them, the more we can use them *qualitatively* to measure the effectiveness of those processes. But if true success is to be measured by the efficacy of an enterprise's performance, we need to relate measures to the *quintessential* nature of that enterprise. In reviewing the place of financial ratios in a model of success for your business we shall be reviewing their characteristics in these three areas – and seeking to identify where they are helpful and where they can be found wanting.

For a fuller illustration of how to apply the 'Three Eff's' in measuring the success of your business, see the tables in Appendix 1.

The Enterprise Stewardship Model

Financial ratios only make sense if they can be related to the processes they are intended to measure. It is therefore important to have a process map for your business that enables you to overlay the key financial ratios you will use to measure its performance.

In constructing a generic-process map of a business we shall use the conventional components of any process: *inputs* to an *activity* in producing an *output* (Figure I.2).

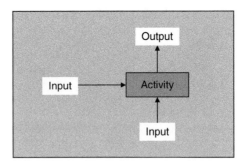

Figure I.2 The components of a process

Although every business is different, the way in which every business develops can be described in a generic set of processes which have been compiled as an Enterprise Stewardship Model (ESM) (Figure I.3). We shall construct this model step by step in Chapter 1 and use it extensively throughout the book.

Again, this model is not prescriptive. Rather it is *descriptive* of the way all enterprises start out and grow. They may not do so consciously, and the model can help identify areas which a business has not consciously addressed. But every business will have needed to at least imitate the steps in the model if it is to become a living enterprise.

The Enterprise Stewardship Model (ESM) was developed to meet the need for clarification and simplicity in managing an enterprise. It has been used in a wide variety of contexts and with a wide variety of audiences. In each case it has proved invaluable as an aid to understanding – and that is what this book is about.

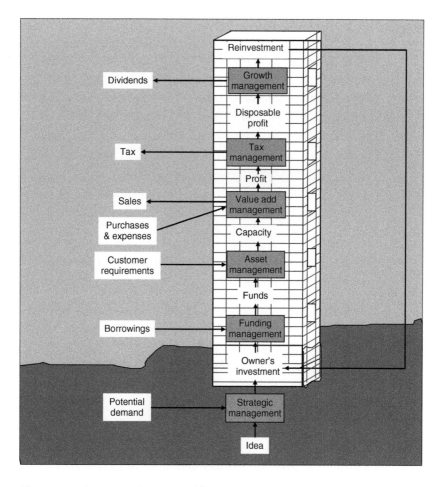

Figure 1.3 The Enterprise Stewardship Model

Some useful tips

1. 'Value and success are in the eye of the beholder'.
   a. There are many 'beholders' (stakeholders) in a business.
   b. Their horizons extend into the future.
   c. There are tangible and intangible elements (and corresponding measures) of value and success.
2. Financial ratios seek to measure the efficiency, effectiveness and efficacy of a business – with varying degrees of success.
3. The Enterprise Stewardship Model describes a generic process for any business or enterprise that can be used for analysis and comparison of processes and their financial performance.

How to use this book

This book is an introduction to financial ratios. As such it lays a foundation of understanding as to what they are trying to achieve, when it is helpful to use them and where their limitations lie. There are a number of weighty tomes written on the subject which define and describe each and every financial ratio 'on the market' (see the Further Reading section at the end of the book for those who wish to study further). As dictionaries of terms they can be very useful, but it is only by starting at our point of need for such measures that we can truly understand their purpose and value to our business. That is where this book starts.

This book is best read as a story, from beginning to end, but falls naturally into three parts:

1. The first part (Chapters 1–2) provides an overview of the key processes in any business and how these processes can be measured with financial ratios.
2. The second part (Chapters 3–7) explores each of these key processes in turn, and examines the risks and benefits involved in using financial ratios as a management tool.
3. The final part (Chapters 8–10) looks at the use of financial ratios from a number of perspectives: where they are used in combination with others, how they can be used in strategic management, and what they represent to different groups of 'stakeholders' within a business.

The CD-ROM that accompanies the book provides some of the illustrations from the book in electronic format; some interactive spreadsheets for calculating ratios in your business and benchmarking them against others; and an opportunity for me to introduce the book and explain how and why it came about. When you insert the CD-ROM in your drive it will show a list of contents which you can navigate by clicking on the items you want to see.

A good rule of construction is that, if a building is to be sturdy and lasting, a third of the cost goes into the ground. The same applies to the use of financial ratios. Time invested in understanding the principles and processes of what we are trying to measure will be time well-spent when selecting and using measures as the basis for decision-making and action.

This book seeks to be a practical guide that can be applied to any enterprise. In writing it I have drawn on my experience in financial management in the manufacturing and financial services sectors and in consultancy across a range of sectors. Indeed the model on which it is based has been applied to both commercial and non-commercial enterprises. I trust it will prove helpful in enabling you to define your own unique model of success and maximize the value and success you seek.

How to maximise value and success

1. Define what you mean by value and success in your business.
2. Use financial ratios as a guide and not a trap.
3. Consider quantitative measures alongside qualitative and quintessential ones.

Caveat

The principles presented in this book apply generally to all enterprises everywhere. However, where specific examples are given of tax and accounting treatment, particularly in Chapter 6 on tax management, these are based on regulations in the UK.

All financial terms used in this book are in line with CIMA *Official Terminology* (see Further Reading). The term 'Inland Revenue' is used to represent organisations like H M Revenue & Customs (HMRC) in the UK or Internal Revenue Service in the USA.

No responsibility for loss occasioned to any person acting or refraining from action as a result of the material in this publication can be accepted by CIMA Publishing, the author or publishers.

Apologia

For simplicity, the pronoun 'he' has been used extensively to refer to a generic term, such as an 'owner' or 'customer' without implying any preference to gender.

PART ONE

The Role of Financial Ratios

Creating value – a model of success

> **Key challenges**
>
> 1. What gives rise to a business or enterprise?
> 2. What is the underlying process of any business or enterprise?
> 3. How does a business create value?

Introduction

The ultimate test of the success of an enterprise is the value that it creates. An enterprise which destroys value, or adds value to one or more group of stakeholders only at the expense of another is unlikely to survive for long. So how can we best monitor the value that an enterprise is creating and how can we assess the benefit that is being shared among its participants? Financial ratios are a crude attempt to do this. But what is the underlying process that they are seeking to measure and what significance can they have for the health and long-term success of an enterprise?

What is needed is a model which sets out the generic process for an enterprise, but over which we can superimpose the unique characteristics of a specific business – including yours – and over which we can map the key financial ratios. In this way we could see how they link together and where and when they can be useful in monitoring progress. In this chapter we will construct such a model through tracing the process of value creation. This will give us a framework for measuring it in the next chapter

Strategic management

What is the first thing one needs in order to start an enterprise? Many people will suggest 'money'. But before such a basic resource can be put to use there needs to be a purpose for it. Thus the very first thing required to launch an enterprise must be an idea that gives rise to that purpose. Companies are encouraged to define their 'vision' – one that can be a guiding force for management and employees in steering their business. Often this is not an exercise in creating a new idea but in recognising and, if necessary, adapting the original vision that gave birth to the existing business.

An idea may appear very creative to the person who first thought of it. However, value is in the eye of the beholder. Therefore, if the benefit it promises to deliver is to be received by others, it is they who will determine its true value. At the same time, 'Everyone has ideas. The best ideas are mine; the worst are other people's that involve me in doing something'. This is the sort of saying that could be attributed to Confucius and reminds us of the need to share our ideas with others and win their support in order to realise them – and realise them to the full.

And so the first thing to do with an idea is to see if anyone else also thinks it is a good idea. Ultimately it will only create value if others see a benefit from it and are willing to sacrifice something in return, typically money, to receive it. This process forms the very foundations of an enterprise. It involves three key elements: careful examination of the idea itself for its intrinsic value; market research to assess its instrumental value; and design and testing to establish how it might be delivered in practice. We shall look at these elements more closely when we consider the strategic use of financial ratios in Chapter 9. For now we will give the label 'strategic management' to this first step in the process (Figure 1.1).

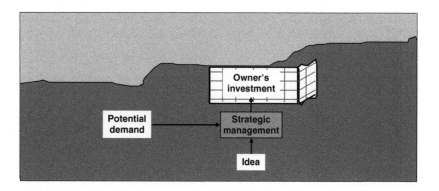

Figure 1.1 Strategic management

Funding management

It is only when others see our idea as beneficial to them that we should be prepared to 'invest' in it ourselves beyond the effort we have expended in the strategic management process. This is some-times the hardest decision of all to take – to accept that an idea will not add value and therefore must be rejected and laid to rest. However, provided we have articulated our idea effectively and there is sufficient potential demand (these being the two inputs to this process) the natural outcome (that is, output) of this process is that the originator, or owner, of the idea should be prepared to commit further to it – and invest in it.

As we are addressing the use of financial ratios, this model may be described using the medium of money, in which case we would naturally envisage the owner's investment being drawn from his bank account. However, just as financial ratios are an expression of the relationship between things that are often intangible, so the investment required by the originator of an idea may be far more than the money he puts into it. It may require his, or her, own reputation to endorse it. It will certainly require energy and enthusiasm to carry it through. And so an owner is likely to invest – and put at stake – something of themselves beyond their tangible assets when they come to launch their enterprise. We now see something visible appearing above the surface of the ground.

Unfortunately, nine times out of ten we don't have all the resources we need to realise an idea ourselves. Whether it is funds, reputation, contacts or whatever, we are likely to need to 'borrow' from others in order to generate the resources required. To use the language of finance, we shall call this process 'funding management' (Figure 1.2). It will require us again to share our idea with others

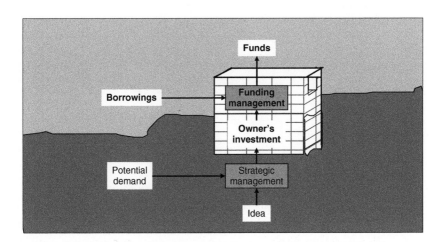

Figure 1.2 Funding management

so that they can see its potential benefits. Only then will they be prepared to accept any risks of investing their own resources in return for promised rewards. This provides the basis for the borrowing contract. Under it individuals or institutions are prepared to lend money to an enterprise in return for interest pending the repayment of their original loan.

Asset management

At this point we have secured the funds that we anticipated we would require to launch our idea into an enterprise. Now we need to consider how best to deploy them. This involves converting funds into assets: the premises for our activity, the people who will carry it out and all the infrastructure required to support it. We shall call this third stage in our model 'asset management' (Figure 1.3).

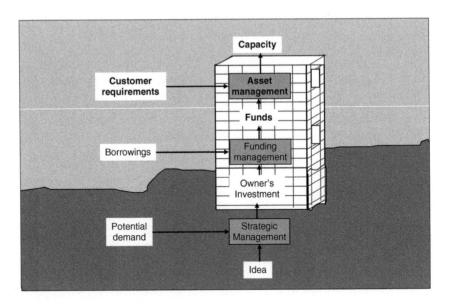

Figure 1.3 Asset management

When investing in assets it is crucial to consider the interests of customers. The relationship with customers and their demand for the goods or services of a company is influenced by a number of factors: the choice of location from which to sell or deliver to them, the selection of staff to serve them, and the design of equipment to respond to changing requirements.

It is also important to recognise the requirements of other stakeholders when establishing and managing an asset base for a business. For it is in meeting their diverse requirements that the effectiveness of those assets in adding value and contributing to long-term success is determined. Since most assets are expected to be of use over a period of time, it is important to consider stakeholder requirements over a similar time frame. There are many methods of investment appraisal which seek to determine the economic return of investing in an asset over its useful life. We shall look at some of these methods in Chapter 7. However, there are a number of weaknesses in any attempt to make an evaluation purely on the basis of financial return. These weaknesses are similar to those inherent in the use of financial ratios.

One weakness stems from any attempt to value 'human assets'. This may appear a derogatory term to describe the people with whom we work and upon whom we rely for the success of our business. The term merely reflects the crude nature of attempts to do so. It has become a cliché that 'our people are our greatest asset'. But there has been little progress in expressing their value to the business in financial terms. It is therefore ironic that a company's 'greatest asset' rarely appears on the balance sheet, unless as potential transfer fees for football clubs. Indeed it more commonly appears as a liability in anticipation of redundancy costs. We shall return to this weakness, amongst others, in Chapter 4 when reviewing financial ratios which seek to measure the effectiveness of such assets.

Thus employees, as well as being key assets themselves, will have their own requirements for assets of the company which they need to do their jobs. The nature and accessibility of those assets will prove important in attracting and retaining quality staff.

In establishing and maintaining an asset base there are other stakeholders who need to be considered beside customers and employees. In order to benefit from supply chain economies and faster response times, companies are drawn to integrating their operations more closely with suppliers. Thus while companies should be recognising the needs of their customers in the supply chain, companies are well advised to consider their suppliers before making investment decisions. Such decisions could inhibit suppliers and create additional costs for them which might only backfire for the company. Managed collaboratively, suppliers could benefit from such decisions and in turn share those benefits with the company.

Finally, central and local Government, as well as non-governmental groups, seek to protect the environment by applying regulations and other forms of control. If companies pollute the environment or waste natural resources they can be penalised for not taking due heed of the interests of the local community in the way that they manage their assets.

Value add management

Up to this point nothing has actually been produced. It has all been planning and organising. What has been created is a capability, or 'capacity', to produce and deliver those goods and services that represent the tangible outcome of our idea or vision. Now the enterprise is in a position to add value to the assets in which it has invested time, effort and financial resources.

The process of adding value implies taking something of potential value and adding to it. A company is invariably one link in a chain of supply. It is often difficult to define the beginning and end of such chains. It may appear to be the first link, for example in extracting raw materials from their natural source. However, even in this case, for instance in foodstuffs or dairy farming, the supply chain can be seen to stretch back to before the harvest of grain or slaughter of animals to the provision of fertilisers or animal feed.

Similarly the final link may not be obvious. Customers themselves often provide it through an act of self-service, whether it be filling their cars up with petrol supplied at the pump or putting together their easy-to-assemble furniture unit.

And so the process of adding value involves the utilisation of assets that a business manages as well as the consumption of goods and services. In financial terms the latter are a firm's purchases and expenses. This is how they are described, as inputs to the process of 'value add management' in our model (Figure 1.4).

If the value received by the customer exceeds the value of purchases, expenses and any reduction in the value of assets resulting from their use, the business can be considered to have added value overall. The mechanism by which this value is then shared between the business and its customers is the selling price. The selling price divides the added value between parties. For the customer the price should represent a perceived level of financial sacrifice less than

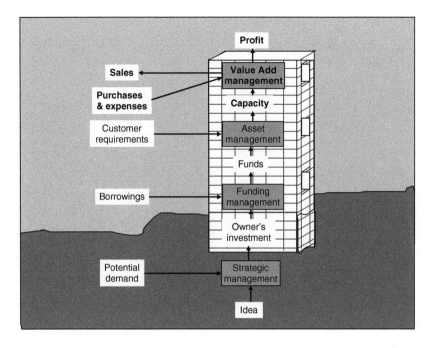

Figure 1.4 Value add management

the benefit he receives. For the company the price should represent a level of financial reward greater than the cost of providing it. It is this mechanism that produces a profit or loss for the enterprise. It is also the mechanism that results in a satisfied or dissatisfied customer.

Pricing is therefore the mechanism which shares the value added by an enterprise between that enterprise and its customers. Price setting does not necessarily require the maximum price that a customer will accept. It may be more important to establish a level and structure of pricing that will achieve a volume of transactions and quality of relationship with customers that is sustainable and will enable the business to grow in the future.

Tax management

Once a profit has been made, the Inland Revenue has first call on it. Just as you and I may receive wages or a salary upon which we must pay income tax, so a company is required to share its profit with the community at large through the payment of corporation tax. This represents an output from the process of 'tax management' in our model (Figure 1.5) and what is left is at the disposal of the enterprise.

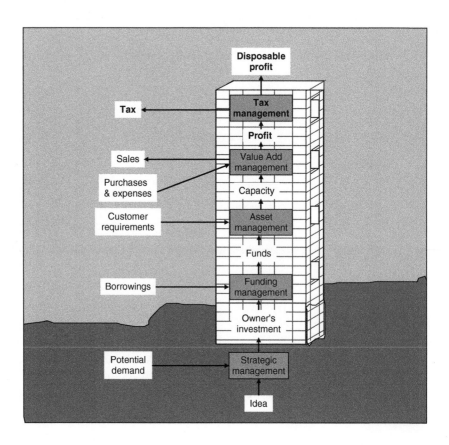

Figure 1.5 Tax management

Despite the uniform rates of corporation tax (with specific reductions for small companies), a company's accounts rarely reflect that rate applying to their declared level of gross profit.

This is a result of the process of tax management within the company. Certain elements of revenue may not incur tax, certain elements of cost may not be allowable against tax and the timing of tax payments may not coincide with the declaration of profits on which they are assessed. As a consequence the 'effective rate' of tax paid by a company can be significantly different from the standard rate, making an equally significant effect on the level of disposable profit available after deduction of tax.

Growth management

A company can do one of two things with the disposable profit that is left after the deduction of tax. It can distribute it to shareholders as a reward for their investment, or it can keep it. The normal vehicle for distributing profits to shareholders is through a dividend. Profits that are not distributed are retained by the company for future use. These might be retained for future dividends in order to maintain a flow of income for shareholders. Alternatively they are available for the further investment of resources in the firm. Either way, they represent an addition to the 'owner's investment' at the base of our model and are shown as part of shareholder equity – as 'retained earnings' – on a company's balance sheet. In this way they provide a circular flow of incoming funds to supplement any new investment provided by new or existing shareholders.

The decision as to whether and how much to distribute in the form of dividends may appear to be a simple one. However it is key in determining the future growth potential of an enterprise. Retained profits can provide direct reinvestment in the business. However, if these are insufficient for the company's growth requirements it may seek an injection of funds from outside. In this case the level of income provided to existing shareholders in dividend payments will influence their preparedness to invest further in the company. Similarly, prospective new investors will regard this as a key factor in influencing their decision whether to invest in the company for the first time. As it has a key bearing on a company's ability to grow in the future, we shall call this part of the process, 'growth management' (Figure 1.6).

However, both an enterprise's potential for growth and its requirement to fund that growth ultimately arise from the foundations of our model. This is where the firm's original idea, or its current expression of that vision, resides. For a company's opportunity for long-term growth will be determined by the quality of its strategic management. This will include the extent to which potential demand has been anticipated and how well the core vision of the enterprise has adapted to changes in the market or technical circumstances.

A company's ability to fund that growth will in turn be determined by the availability of retained profits or the willingness of new or existing shareholders to provide fresh investment to the company.

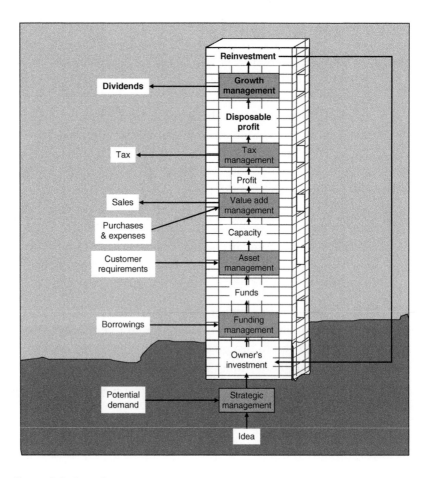

Figure 1.6 Growth management

Responding to key challenges

1. The first thing required for an enterprise is an idea.
2. A business or enterprise can be described by six key processes:
   i. Strategic management
   ii. Funding management
   iii. Asset management
   iv. Value add management
   v. Tax management
   vi. Growth management
3. A business creates value by taking something of potential value and adding to it.

Now that we have introduced these key processes within the Enterprise Stewardship Model, we will refer to them throughout without special designation. However, wherever the above terms are used within this book, they refer consistently to the steps described in the model.

In the next chapter this provides the framework for understanding the role of financial ratios. It provides a picture for seeing what they are trying to achieve and how they can best be used to measure the performance of the business and steer it to success.

How to maximise value and success

1. Describe the original vision for your business and how it has developed.
2. Recognise the whole process required to create value and success.
3. Focus on total value rather than that part of it that accrues to any one stakeholder.

Measuring value – the origin of financial ratios

Key challenges

1. How can we measure the performance of a business using financial ratios?
2. How do financial ratios relate to one another?
3. How can we check the integrity of a set of financial ratios?

Introduction

It is one thing to have a business model. It is something else to use that model to maximise value and manage a business successfully.

In chapter 1 the model was constructed. It can now be examined to see how it can be used as a tool of management. In particular it will be used to show how financial ratios can help monitor the business and steer it to success.

The model reflects a process – one that any entrepreneur will follow, consciously or unconsciously, in building a business. It also comprises a series of sub-processes. These help to break down the journey from ideas to success. They also provide steps along the way to measure progress and indicate corrective action.

Any process comprises an activity prompted by inputs and resulting in outputs (see Figure I.2).

To be a value added process the activity has to add value to the inputs in delivering the output. If we can measure the relationship in value between the inputs and outputs we can then have a measure of the extent to which the activity has added value. This is the basis of conventional process measurement. Our process is no exception, and, as we can see from our model (Figure 2.1), it comprises a series of inputs and outputs rising vertically as well as a number of inputs and outputs flowing laterally. Outputs that rise vertically within the overall process (i.e. remain within the building) form inputs to the next process; while outputs that flow out of the building represent 'leaks' and inputs that flow into the building represent 'injections'.

It is now time to follow the journey step by step, plotting where financial ratios can provide a guide – and where they need to be used with care. At times we shall examine how effectively an output is created from a given level of input. At others we shall examine

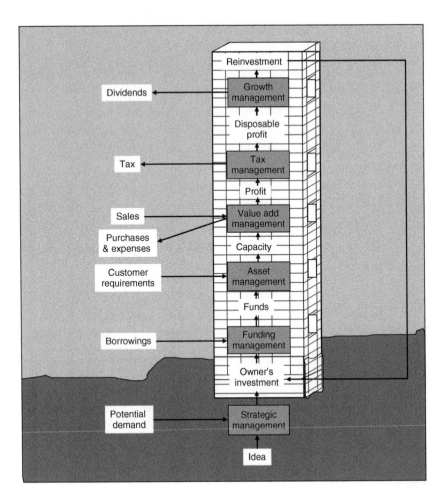

Figure 2.1 Business as a process for measurement

how effectively two inputs are combined to produce a given output. But in each case we shall use a financial metric – money – as the common unit of measurement so that both inputs and outputs can be expressed in the same terms for comparison. We shall then look to see how, just as the model builds together into one holistic process, the financial ratios that have been constructed relate to one another and combine to form an overview of the whole process.

In plotting the financial ratios for each process, the components of these ratios will be drawn from a company's financial statements – its balance sheet and profit and loss account. We shall not explore the validity or accuracy of such statements at this stage but revisit these issues when examining ratios in more detail in Chapters 3–7. For the benefit of those unfamiliar with the terms or who may appreciate a reminder, Appendix 2 illustrates how the components of these ratios are derived from a company's financial statements.

The value of strategy

The first stage in the construction of a business is strategic management – creating the foundations. At this stage nothing is visible above the ground and therefore nothing is measurable in that sense. That does not mean that the value of strategic management cannot be assessed. Its value will become evident in the degree, depth and resilience of the *commitment* made to the business that arises from how profound, distinctive and enduring is the *vision*. Figure 2.2 illustrates this relationship.

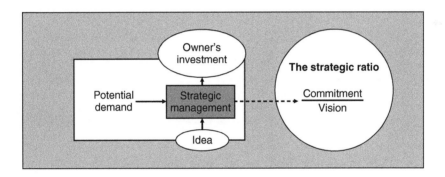

Figure 2.2 The strategic ratios

It is important to acknowledge that the foundations contain properties which are hidden from the naked eye. The strategic management process encapsulates, in concept, the entire edifice of an enterprise. This process is explored more deeply in Chapter 9 which examines how the proof of the work at this stage becomes evident in the construction at subsequent stages. So now we will turn our attention to what can be seen 'above the ground'.

The gearing ratio

The first evidence of construction appears at the point of investment by the originator – or owner – of the idea. However, as already acknowledged in the last chapter, the owner does not usually have all the resources required to realise this idea. He invariably needs to borrow from others. How effectively he does so will depend on the strength of his idea and the confidence which he generates in potential lenders. For every pound (or euro, dollar, etc) that the owner puts in, we can see how much others are prepared to lend.

Of course the terms of lending between different companies and their lenders may be quite different. In particular the rate of interest which lenders are prepared to accept for the risk and inconvenience of being without their cash may cover a wide range. This will be examined more closely in Chapter 3.

Another way of viewing the relationship of inputs and outputs in a process is to take one of the inputs and see how effectively it uses the other input in producing the output. In this case we could take the amount of the owner's investment and the level of borrowings and see how effectively one is 'geared up' by the other to generate the total resources produced.

The funding management process uses the term *gearing ratio* to express this relationship. This gearing ratio is convention-ally expressed as the amount of total funding – including funds raised from borrowings – generated from a volume of shareholders' investment.

If we turn to the financial statements of a company we shall find these two elements identified on the balance sheet as *total liabilities* and *equity capital*. The comparison of these two elements, in the form of a ratio, Total Liabilities/Equity, provides what is known as the company's gearing ratio (Figure 2.3). It measures the total amount of funds generated from a given level of shareholder investment.

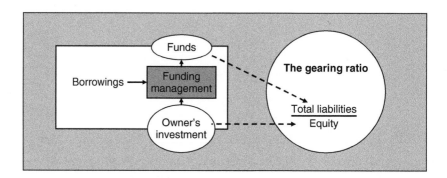

Figure 2.3 The gearing ratio

The asset turnover ratio

We now turn to the next process in our model of success, *asset management*. A level of resources has been generated in the form of funds and the process of asset management converts these funds into tangible – and intangible – assets. We are seeking to measure how effectively the enterprise selects and manages these assets in optimising its capability to add value through its goods or services. This capability may again take tangible and intangible forms and it may not all be utilised. But one way of measuring its outcome is the amount of goods or services actually produced or sold – in financial terms, the revenue generated.

Thus we have the basis for a measurement. The effectiveness of this process – how well a company utilises its assets to produce goods and services – can now be measured by comparing the amount of output (or revenue) generated from the available assets (Figure 2.4).

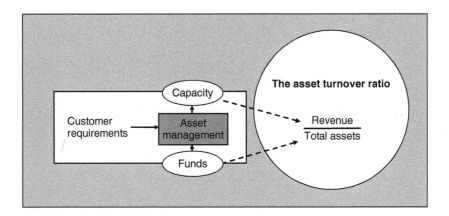

Figure 2.4 The asset turnover ratio

The revenue of a company is declared in its *profit and loss account*. Its assets are shown on its *balance sheet*. We shall look at the components of its assets (and examine the issue of intangible assets) in Chapter 4. But for current purposes we will take the entire asset base, or *total assets*, as listed in a company's balance sheet.

The financial ratio which is therefore used to measure the effectiveness with which a business 'turns over' its assets is Revenue/Total Assets and is known as the *asset turnover ratio*.

The profit margin

The asset turnover ratio measures the value of goods and services generated from the total assets of the business. However, as recognised earlier, the process of adding value consumes goods and services as well as drawing from the value of those assets. Thus the share of value added which the company receives is the difference between the total cost of goods and services sold and the price which the customer pays for them.

The company's share of value added is represented by its profit. The *profit margin* measures the effectiveness with which this profit is generated from revenue through the value add management process. Both profit and revenue are to be found in the profit and loss account, and the profit margin is the ratio of one to the other (Figure 2.5).

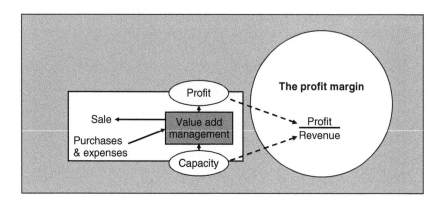

Figure 2.5 The profit margin

The effective tax rate

It has been shown how the value that has been added by the enterprise has been shared with the customer. However, the share that is initially received by the company, being the difference between the cost of providing its product or service and the price received for it, has other calls on it.

The first call on a company's profit is from the tax authorities who demand a share of profits in order to provide services through central government. Local government will have already gathered its income through business rates which are treated as expenses in the process of value add management.

While corporation tax is levied at a standard rate (or on a sliding scale for smaller companies), examination of most company's accounts will reveal that the proportion of profits paid in tax does not often equate to that rate. This is a result of various tax regulations. Some allow a company to avoid paying tax altogether on certain activities or for the use of certain resources while others allow a company to defer its payment of tax to a period other than that in which the profit was earned.

This process of tax management mirrors that of personal tax management whereby tax is assessed and deducted from personal income to leave disposable income. We shall therefore call the output from this process for a company *disposable profit.*

The accounting term for this is net after tax (NAT) profit and can be compared to the level of profit before tax is levied – net before tax (NBT) profit. The ratio gives a measure of the effectiveness of the company in 'managing' its own effective tax rate. While the use of the term 'effective tax rate' normally applies to the ratio of tax assessed to profit, we shall use the same term here to describe the ratio of profit before and after tax has been deducted (Figure 2.6).

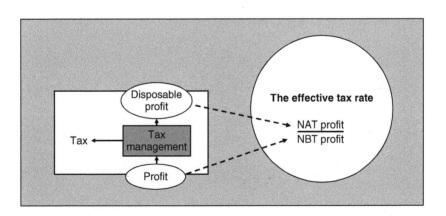

Figure 2.6 The effective tax rate

The payout ratio

Now that we have determined the amount of profit available to the company after taxation, the final call on it is from shareholders who seek an income from their (equity) investment. The proportion of (NAT) profits that are retained by the company for reinvestment is known as the *retention ratio* (Figure 2.7a) and we shall call the remaining proportion that is distributed to shareholders, the *payout ratio* (Figure 2.7b).

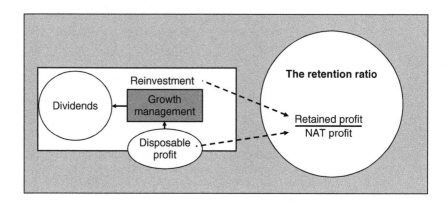

Figure 2.7a The retention ratio

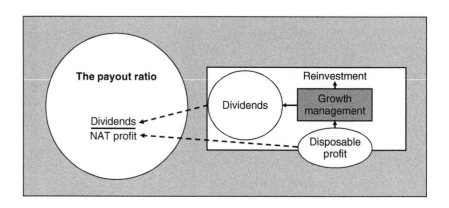

Figure 2.7b The payout ratio

Composite ratios

Having reached the summit of the model and tracked the circular flow of value and funds which enable sustenance and future growth, the five major components of the process which an enterprise follows have been plotted (Figure 2.8).

Each of these components can be broken down into smaller elements for more detailed examination and this is done in Chapters 3–7.

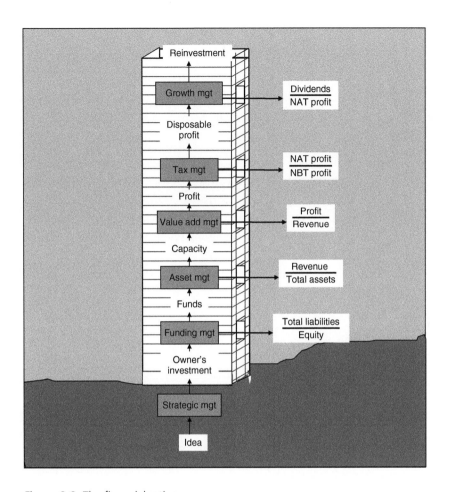

Figure 2.8 The financial ratios

However, it is also helpful to measure the performance of an enterprise at a more summary level. One way of achieving this is to create composite financial ratios from those of the individual adjacent processes.

The arithmetic involved in creating composite financial ratios across more than one process is as follows. A composite ratio can be derived by multiplying the individual ratios together from the processes being consolidated. In algebraic form an example is

$$A/B \times B/C = A/C$$

This results from the fact that the denominator (B) of the first expression (A/**B**) is the same as the numerator of the second expression (**B**/C) and is therefore cancelled out in the multiplication, leaving the numerator of the first expression (**A**/B) and the denominator of the second expression (B/**C**).

As a by-product of consolidating the financial ratios for sub-processes, this exercise demonstrates the integrity of the model by confirming that the whole is a product of the parts.

As shown in Chapter 8, this is not just an elegant mathematical exercise to add to the tool-kit of financial ratios at our disposal. It is helpful when combining together certain components of the total business process – those for which we wish to have meaningful measures that can be helpful in managing success in a business. In compiling these higher-level measurements, we will start with the processes which lie at the very heart of the enterprise, and work outwards, step by step, to the extremities of the model (Figure 2.9).

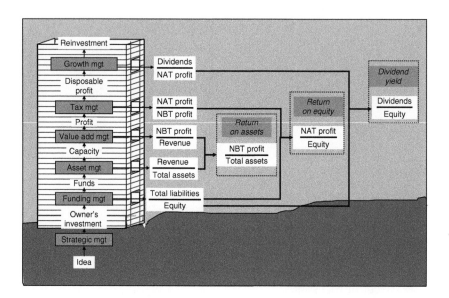

Figure 2.9 The composite ratios

The return on assets ratio

The two core processes within an enterprise are the management of its assets and the delivery of value to its customers. We have derived financial ratios – the *asset turnover ratio* and the *profit margin* – as measures for these two processes, but it would be helpful to have one measure that spans both and that expresses the amount of profit that is being generated from the funds, or assets, at the company's disposal.

By multiplying together the profit margin and the asset turnover ratio we are able to derive such a measure. Thus, following the logic of the algebraic example above, NBT profit / Revenue × Revenue /Assets = NBT profit /Assets, In the jargon of the accountants, profit is here described as that element of value which is 'returned' to the company, and the ratio has therefore acquired the title *return on assets*. It is illustrated as spanning the two core processes of *asset management* and *value add management* in our model (see Figure 2.9).

The return on equity ratio

The return on assets ratio is a very useful internal measure of the amount of profit a company is generating from its assets. However, external shareholders want to see how effectively the company is using their investment, as opposed to borrowed funds, in view of the risk to which they have committed that capital.

In order to identify the return that shareholders achieve on their investment we therefore need to broaden our perspective beyond the return on assets and take in the processes of funding management and tax management. The funding management process distinguishes the funding provided by shareholders' equity from that raised by long-term borrowing; while the tax management process distinguishes the share of profit which is available to shareholders from that which is due to the Inland Revenue.

Using the same method of arithmetic as above, we can derive a composite financial ratio that spans these processes: from funding management to tax management. As the two central processes have already been combined into one – the return on assets – we can multiply it by the two peripheral ones – the gearing ratio and effective tax rate – to derive the broader composite we are seeking.

The product formed is

NAT profit /*NBT profit* × *NBT Profit*/*Total assets*

× *Total liabilities*/**Equity**

As the balance sheet of any enterprise requires that its *total assets* equal its *total liabilities*, these two, along with *NBT profit*, cancel out to leave **NAT profit/Equity** (see Figure 2.9).

This ratio is given the potentially confusing term *'return on equity'*. The potential source of confusion lies in the fact that the 'return' in 'return on equity' referred to here is the return available to shareholders – net profit *after* tax (NAT). It is not to be confused with the 'return' in 'return on assets' which is net profit *before* tax (NBT).

The dividend yield

The return on equity ratio measures the amount of profit a company generates for the benefit of its shareholders. As such it encompasses four of the five key processes in our business model. If shareholders wish to know how much they are receiving in hard cash, through dividends, in return for their investment, they need to include the decision at the heart of the growth management process. This third composite ratio, called the *dividend yield*, is therefore derived from multiplying the payout ratio by the return on equity: **Dividends**/NAT profit × NAT profit/**Equity** (see Figure 2.9). The resulting ratio of **Dividends/Equity** describes how much hard cash the shareholder's original investment is yielding at the original (or 'nominal') value of the shares.

The composite test

Composite ratios have now been derived which encompass an ever increasing scope of activities in which an enterprise is engaged. These activities extend from the initial investment by an owner or shareholder to the provision of dividends to that shareholder as a tangible reward for such an investment. In doing so, we have used simple arithmetic to derive composite ratios from the component ratios within the model.

These composite ratios provide measures to assess the broader scopes of the management process. By testing the mathematical integrity of the model, the reader can be confident that the model, for all its brevity and simplicity, is comprehensive and suitably robust for further examination and exploration.

Responding to key challenges

1. Financial ratios can be used to measure the performance of each key process within a business – individually or collectively.
2. Financial ratios link together in the same way as the processes they are measuring.
3. The financial ratios mapped over the Enterprise Stewardship Model can be tested arithmetically, as well as conceptually, by the 'composite test' for their scope and integrity.

We shall embark on this closer examination of the model, in order to reveal insights it gives into the place for financial ratios, in Chapters 3–7. We shall return to explore the use of the composite ratios more closely in Chapter 8.

How to maximise value and success

1. Look behind the numbers to the *underlying process*.
2. Identify what aspects of value and success financial ratios *can't measure*.
3. Assess the relationship between value and risk for all stakeholders.

PART TWO

Understanding Financial Ratios

Funding management –
the gearing ratio

Key challenges

1. How much do we need in order to finance a business?
2. Where should it come from?
3. What will it cost?

The first time that financial ratios become relevant in a new enterprise is if and when the original owner or entrepreneur recognises that their own funds are insufficient and therefore seek to raise the funds they need from other sources. It is only at this stage that the enterprise starts taking tangible form and appears 'above the ground' in the model. However, even if an enterprise can be launched without borrowing, it is often a consequence of success that the owner wishes to expand at some later date beyond their own capacity to fund it. It is at this point that they turn to others for help.

This process represents the first step in the realisation of the idea behind an enterprise. It is therefore important that it is constructed in line with the strategic plans for the business, so that the structure can be properly supported. Where there are a number of people and/or organisations contributing to the funding – whether their individual status be as shareholders, debenture holders or other long-term lenders – their relationship to one another represents a partnership of interests.

The respective interests of these partners need to be recognised. They need to be brought into harmony with each other and the needs of the business. 'Gearing' is a rather mechanistic term for this, but it is the one given to the relationship between shareholders and other sources of long-term borrowing in terms of the respective contributions made by their funds (Figure 3.1).

Key questions

In order to manage the funding process effectively the three key questions above need to be answered. To repeat:

1. How much is needed?
2. Where will it come from?
3. What will it cost?

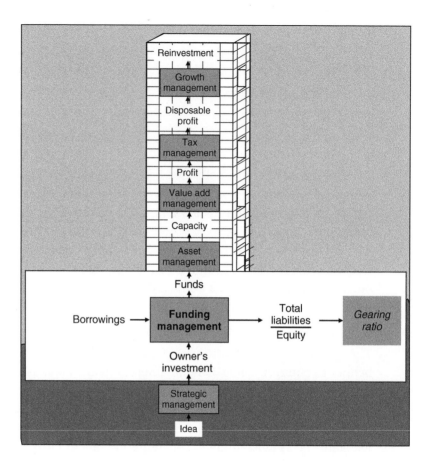

Figure 3.1 Funding management

The answers to these questions depend on a number of factors: how the owner seeks to realise their idea; the nature of the risks and rewards involved in realising it; and the nature of the market and industry they are operating in. The value that financial ratios bring to this process is in measuring the effectiveness of the owners: how will they generate financial support for their idea; the balance between risks and rewards for each party; and the cost to the business of the respective sources of funding.

How much is needed?

The minimum amount of funds required is that which is required to support the enterprise at its minimum sustainable scale. There may be a critical mass of investment required in terms of premises, equipment and working capital below which the enterprise cannot start or continue to function. This will determine the minimum level of funding required. Beyond this, as the enterprise grows, there will be increasing levels of scale at which the enterprise could function at increasing levels of efficiency and effectiveness. In turn, operating at a larger scale can enable its products or services to reach a wider market and thereby maximise its efficacy.

The scale of funding required should be calculated during the strategic management process when these factors are first envisaged and tested out (see Chapter 9). It will be driven by the demands for the asset base from which the business is planned to operate.

Assets can usefully be divided into two groups. There are those from which value is realised over a significant period of time (for accounting purposes, and rather arbitrarily, chosen as being in excess of a year). These are known as *fixed assets*. And there are those from which value is realised over a shorter period (using the same arbitrary dividing line of a year). These are known as *current assets*.

Buildings and equipment which are bought by a company (or for which the right to use them over a period longer than a year is secured in some way) are examples of fixed assets. Stock and debts owed to the company which are expected to be paid for within a year, are examples of current assets.

The matching principle

The main objective of the funding-management process is to ensure the long-term financial viability of the enterprise. It is therefore primarily concerned with the funding of long-term, or fixed, assets. But it also needs to provide for the funding of short term, or current, assets where the requirement for this is ongoing.

For if short-term assets were to be entirely funded by short-term funds (or *liabilities*) such as money owed to suppliers (creditors) or to the bank in the form of an overdraft, then the business would be vulnerable if the balance was upset for some reason so that it was unable to pay its suppliers or its employees. This could be as a result of bad debts from customers or the withdrawal of overdraft facilities by the bank and in turn result in running out of cash, or illiquidity.

Illiquidity can also arise from an apparently positive development. As a business grows, increased levels of purchases and inventories put more demand on funds. If this outpaces the flow of cash received through sales – especially if these are on credit – the business can run out of cash. This is known as *overtrading* and is a common cause of insolvency arising from the apparent success (but actual mismanagement) of a business.

It is a well-known axiom that businesses do not go bankrupt because of making losses; they go bankrupt because they run out of cash. Witness the ability of some start-ups to survive despite heavy losses while established firms can go bust following an ambitious expansion programme.

It has therefore become an important principle in funding an enterprise that long-term assets should be funded by long-term sources of funds. Also any ongoing shortfall of funding short-term assets that cannot be met, within foreseeable parameters of risk, by short-term sources of funds should also be funded from long-term sources. It is a rule of thumb that a ratio of 2:1 between current assets and current liabilities (known as the *current ratio*) is considered healthy for most businesses. It is an important indicator of liquidity – the actual level that is appropriate will depend on the circumstances of the market and terms of trade with customers and suppliers. A common ratio adopted as a stricter guide is the *acid test ratio* which compares the level of cash and bank deposits available at no notice to the level of current liabilities. In other words, in the acid test of current liabilities being called in at short notice, could the business meet them from readily available sources?

Where will the funds come from?

This leads naturally to the second question – the source of funding for the business and the terms upon which such funding is obtained.

The two key considerations in determining the appropriate sources of funding are the length of time the funding is required and the level of risk involved. This covers the twin principles of matching – over time and between risks and rewards. Different assets will present different combinations of risk and reward. It is important to ensure that they are complementary within themselves. But it is also important to match their respective profiles with the corresponding requirements and expectations of those who are providing the funding for them.

Forms of borrowing

When considering assets that are required long term in the business, such as premises or equipment, there is a variety of potential ways of financing them. For instance the long-term right to occupy buildings and premises might be obtained by purchasing the freehold or acquiring a lease on them. In the former case the freehold might be best financed by investment in shares (or 'equity') by the owners if the facilities are likely to be needed as long as the enterprise exists.

Alternatively a lease might be more appropriate if requirements and circumstances could change significantly in a 5–10-year timescale. This might call for a relocation or alternative method of servicing the business. The lease may provide for a combination of an upfront price for the purchase of the right to lease as well as an ongoing rental during the lease period (the rental being fixed or variable subject to negotiation).

In this case a fixed-term loan for the purchase price over a matching period might be appropriate. At the same time the income from the asset should match the profile of repayments for servicing the loan. Indeed, provided the facility is genuinely adding value in servicing the ultimate customer – and this is realised in cash – it will effectively be self-financing.

Financing plant and machinery by way of a lease is often an attractive form of financing for this reason. We will not go into the exact vagaries here of how different forms of lease are recognised as capital or operating leases and therefore how they are recognised in the accounts, but the funding principle applies however they are accounted.

It is the matching principle which is at the heart of the funding management process, and it is this which enables the owner to apply a multiplier to the funds which they are able to contribute themselves in order to meet the wider requirements of the business.

Forms of ownership

The financing requirements of a business can be very varied and it is worth distinguishing between different forms of funding that can be provided by the owners themselves.

The various forms of legal identity for businesses, from *sole trader* enterprises to *partnerships* and *limited companies*, offer different structures for setting the boundaries for personal liability while enabling the owners to benefit from the rewards of their enterprise.

However, limited liability on the part of the owners may influence the preparedness of other investors – including those providing short-term credit as suppliers – to risk their own funds when there is limited opportunity to reclaim them in the event of the business itself not generating enough to repay them.

Even before looking to conventional forms of 'borrowings' the owner can seek to share ownership on different terms with others. Some investors may be attracted by being given priority over others in the distribution of the Disposable Profit which becomes available after tax (Chapter 7).

Such shareholders may be prepared to allow limits on the reward they receive in order to receive such priority treatment. In this case a category of ownership can be established for those who hold a 'preference share' whereby they receive their reward first (say 5 per cent of the nominal value of their shares). The company then determines the appropriate reward for those who hold 'ordinary shares' from the profits that are left.

As the risk of lack of sufficient disposable profit to meet even the commitments to preference shareholders increases the more there are of them, so the ratio of after-tax profit to preference share dividend indicates the level of *dividend cover* existing.

In turn, the more preference shareholders there are, the greater the risk – and potential reward – to ordinary shareholders. As the dividend payable to owners of preference shares is fixed, the amount available to ordinary shareholders depends on how much the disposable profit exceeds that fixed amount. 'Gearing' at this more detailed level is indicated by the ratio of preferred share capital to total shareholder equity. The greater the level of risk and rewards to ordinary shareholders, the greater that ratio. Again the degree to which after tax profit 'covers' ordinary share dividends will indicate the level of security for those ordinary shareholders.

There is now a wide variety of forms of ownership that is available to investors. These provide different levels of security and commitment, with attendant risks and rewards. Indeed it is sometimes difficult to distinguish between those who are classed as owners (included as 'equity' on the balance sheet) and those who are regarded as a source of 'long-term borrowing'.

How much will it cost?

The same principle of matching applies when seeking to balance the risks and rewards of the financing arrangement with the requirements of those providing the funding. There are three factors which will determine the level of harmony with which this is achieved.

The first is the level of confidence generated in the lender. This will be greatly influenced by the ability of the owner to convey the viability and potential success of the underlying vision of the enterprise. The second is any specific security offered for the loan, whereby the owner releases a stake in part of the assets of the company as a means of sharing ownership. The third is the amount and form of reward to the lender in consideration for the risk they are taking with their loan. This is largely determined by the rate of interest paid. In this way the owner is sharing the value which has been added from the assets financed by the lender.

Those who provide funds to an enterprise in this way can look to certain ratios for indications of risk and reward from their investment. Just as shareholders look to the level of dividend cover, so those with fixed term/fixed interest-rate loans or debentures may look to the degree to which the interest they receive is covered by profit. While interest expense is an element of cost absorbed during the Value Add process (and charged to the P&L), the ability of the company to pay it is best indicated by the additional 'cover' provided by profits. Thus the ratio of profit to interest expense provides an equivalent indicator of cover for the lender.

In seeking to match the levels and forms of borrowing to requirements, the business itself can measure the cost of such borrowing from the ratio of interest expense to debt. This can be done at different levels to assess the appropriateness of the company's debt structure and methods of servicing it. It can be done for each category of debt, for groups of categories or in total. It can also be instructive to review the ratio of short-term debt to long-term debt – again to assess the appropriateness of the mix in relation to the time horizons of different components of the business plan.

As mentioned earlier, it is sometimes difficult to distinguish in principle between equity and long-term liabilities. Sometimes it is also difficult to distinguish between long- and short-term liabilities. It can even be difficult to determine whether something should be treated as equity or an expense. A vivid example of this is the matter of employee share options. Some argue that they are an element of remuneration and should therefore be expensed, while others argue that they are commitments by the company to issue share capital and should therefore be recognised as equity.

These examples illustrate how difficult it can be to apply the matching principle in practice. However, it is important for those directing the enterprise and managing its funding requirements to constantly review the relationship between the various sources of funds and the relationship between each source and the level of risk and reward it incurs. The various ratios referred to above can help in assessing how appropriate these relationships are so that they might be sustainable in the long term and support the realisation of the underlying vision for the enterprise.

Responding to key challenges

1. A business has a minimum sustainable scale, driven by the demands of the asset base.
2. Funds can be obtained from the owner's investment (equity) and/or from borrowing.
3. The cost of funds will depend on the level of confidence (or risk) held by investors.

How to maximise value and success

1. Make sure your strategic plan describes the scale of funding required at different stages of growth.
2. Make sure the sources of funds are matched with the type of requirements.
3. Make sure funders are receiving an appropriate share of the value added by the enterprise.

Asset management – the asset turnover ratio

Key challenges

1. What assets are most important to a business?
2. How much should we invest in them?
3. How do we assess how well they are used?

Introduction

In the last chapter we addressed the need for companies to fund their long-term assets, together with any potential shortfall in short-term assets which are not covered by short-term liabilities. We now move on to examine the company's management of those assets and how that can best be measured by using financial ratios. This takes us to the second 'floor' of our model and the process of asset management (Figure 4.1).

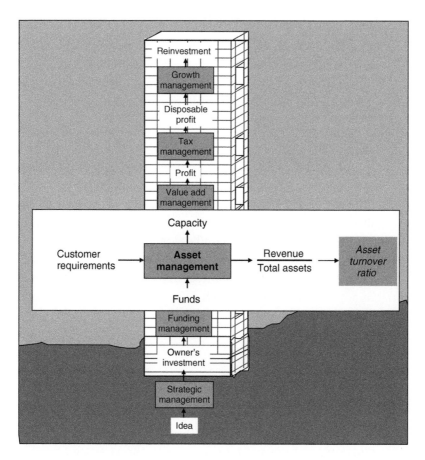

Figure 4.1 Asset management

Asset management is the process of converting funds into assets that have the capacity to produce and deliver the goods or services that the enterprise seeks to provide. More than that, it is the process of managing those assets – both tangible and intangible – so that they fulfil their potential to add value in the most efficient and effective way which is in accord with the purpose and vision of the company.

These three criteria: efficiency, effectiveness and efficacy, are the three dimensions of performance that we identified in the introduction as important to be able to measure. Financial ratios tend to be most helpful in measuring the first two, while efficacy (the ability to produce the results intended) is more difficult to pin down in purely financial terms. We shall illustrate this through the use of financial ratios to measure how well a company manages its assets.

Disaggregating the asset turnover ratio

As discussed in Chapter 2 and illustrated here in Figure 4.1, the asset management process can be measured crudely in financial terms by relating the amount of revenue generated by a company's assets to the amount of money tied up in those assets:

Revenue / Total assets, (known as the asset turnover ratio)

If we use financial ratios to measure a company's asset management performance in more detail, we shall inevitably be influenced by the categories in which they are defined on the balance sheet and in the company's books. However these are invariably limited to tangible assets. The intangible assets of a company are becoming more important as knowledge is becoming an ever more critical and highly valued asset in business. Intangible assets are often the most important source of competitive advantage for a company and its ability to add value.

However, we shall start by addressing tangible assets.

Tangible assets

A company's balance sheet will typically distinguish between fixed and current assets and we can examine the asset turnover ratio (ATR) of a company more closely by breaking these assets down into their component parts.

To facilitate this analysis it is more convenient to look at asset turnover in terms of how long it takes for a given category of assets to be 'turned over' by a firm's revenue. This is the inverse of the ATR and produces the ratio Total assets/Revenue. As we are comparing a 'stock' (assets) to a 'flow' (revenue) the time period in which the 'turnover' is expressed depends on that chosen for the revenue.

A firm's financial statements will usually cover the period of a year's trading. The time it takes to 'turn over' its assets will therefore be expressed as a number of years and/or part of a year. If, however, we calculate the average daily revenue figure and use that, we shall express asset turnover in terms of number of days. As we shall see, this is a more relevant way of expressing it when we get down to some of the component asset groups.

We commence our analysis by expressing the distinction between fixed and current assets with the formula:

Total assets/Revenue =

Current assets/Revenue + Fixed assets/Revenue

These two components can in turn be broken down for further analysis. In the first case, where current assets comprise inventory, debtors and cash:

Current assets/Revenue =

Inventory/Revenue + Debtors/Revenue + Cash/Revenue

and, where fixed assets are made up of buildings, plant and machinery (P & M), and fixtures and fittings (F & F):

Fixed assets/Revenue =

Buildings/Revenue + P & M/Revenue + F & F/Revenue

Thus the external face of our model provides a summarised version of the asset management process within the total business process. If we wish to look closer we can peer through the window of this floor of the building to understand in more detail how the company is managing its assets.

If even more detailed analysis is required, each element can be broken down still further. For instance, the first element of the current asset turnover ratio listed above is the inventory turnover ratio, so that where Total inventory = Raw materials + Work-in-Progress (WIP) + Finished stock, then:

Total inventory/Revenue =

Raw materials/Revenue + WIP/Revenue + Finished stock/Revenue

and so on.

Using the component ratios

This analysis produces a menu and hierarchy of asset categories (as represented in Figure 4.2) which enables an assessment of a company's asset turnover ratio for different components of inventory and at different levels of detail. It also represents a route map to trace the conversion of a firm's funds to its capacity for revenue. The analysis can go deeper, examining the component breakdown of each of these sub-categories for as far as the detailed information is available.

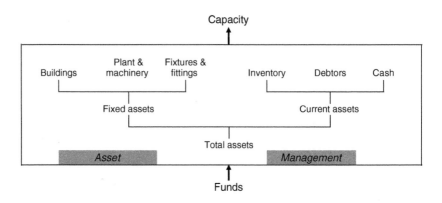

Figure 4.2 Analysis of assets on the balance sheet

For the purposes of this book we shall structure our examination at the second level of analysis. In this way we shall explore the value – and limitations – of purely financial ratios and see how they can be enriched with the use of non-financial ratios and judicious questioning. There is a limit to the real information that financial data on its own can provide. This limit is reached fairly quickly when examining asset categories as defined on the balance sheet.

It applies even earlier when we wish to examine intangible assets that may or may not even be listed there.

Current asset turnover ratios

The inventory turnover ratio

There are a number of reasons why we might want to know how long, on average, our inventory remains in the business before being sold. It indicates how long our cash is being tied up, which may have implications for the cost of borrowings required to fund it (see Chapter 3). It is also likely to take up space, which will incur an occupancy cost. And it invariably absorbs time in supervision and management and therefore labour costs. Like paper in an in-tray, inventory attracts attention, raises anxieties while it is unresolved and calls for the need to justify its existence.

And so the financial implications of inventory represent only one of the reasons for wishing to know how quickly it 'turns over' in the business. Stocks of perishable goods, in either raw material or finished state, may become unusable and therefore a direct cost as 'wastage'. Similarly, finished goods could become obsolete – through changes in fashion or technology – if unsold for too long. In both cases the effectiveness as well as the efficiency of the business is affected and they become value detractors rather than sources of value add.

There are other implications of holding inventory, not all of them negative. Certain levels of inventory may be required to ensure availability for customers. This may extend beyond wishing to ensure that sales are not lost to competitors who are able to provide or deliver faster; it may reflect a core value of the company, that the customer should not be inconvenienced for the sake of expediency. In that case, other measures may be required, such as customer satisfaction or loyalty levels, to assess the efficacy of the company's inventory management policy.

The inventory turnover ratio is usually expressed, as above, in the form:

Revenue/Inventory

where revenue is the total sales for the year.

However sometimes it is more convenient and compelling to express it in its reciprocal form:

Inventory/Revenue

where revenue in this case is calculated as the average daily sales.

In its latter form inventory turnover is expressed as a number of days-equivalent or *inventory days* and describes more explicitly how long it is taking to convert inventory into sales.

Inventory represents just one of those sources of 'capacity' – in this case for making a sale and delivering the goods or services of a business – that the process of asset management in our model is designed to generate from the funds available to it.

Much of the recent enthusiasm for 'just in time' (JIT) production has been to reduce costs associated with holding inventory of raw materials and components. And companies have been keen to adopt Japanese 'kan-ban' techniques and build-to-order principles in manufacturing in order to reduce finished goods stocks. The combination of these two developments has led to the need for an ever closer logistical relationship between suppliers and customers throughout the supply chain (see Chapter 5).

The debtor turnover ratio

There are a number of reasons why we might want to know how long our customers are taking to pay us. Like inventory, debtors are 'cash-in-waiting' and therefore contribute to our funding requirements. But a delay in payment may be a symptom of other problems, such as poor administrative processes or a dissatisfied customer.

Just as the inventory turnover ratio can be expressed as the number of days worth of inventory that is held, so the relationship of revenue to those assets represented by debtors can be expressed as the average number of days before debts are received – variously known as *debtor days* or the *collection period*. Thus:

Debtors / Revenue (per day) = Debtor days (on average)

The number of actual debtor days represented by the level of debt outstanding can be compared against the normal terms of payment required by the company. If the number of debtor days is greater than the terms, this implies an inability or unwillingness on the part of customers to pay on time. Inability to pay can result from lack of liquidity on their part or quality deficiencies in billing while an unwillingness to pay can result from quality problems in the goods or services themselves. Thus, apart from being a source of demand for funding for the company, the debtor turnover ratio can indicate problems elsewhere. Like many of the other ratios it answers some questions and serves to prompt further questions to discover the causes of the symptoms it is showing.

The cash turnover ratio

Cash is classified as the most liquid of a company's current assets. As such it should also be managed efficiently, effectively and for the right purposes. Idle cash does not earn income unless it is converted, at least to short-term deposits earning interest. However it can serve a useful purpose as a buffer to enable the settlement of debts to suppliers and lenders where the flow of settlements from customers and other debtors does not coincide. Thus the more these two flows can be made coincidental, the lower the demand for a buffer and the more efficient the use of cash.

However, as we have seen with the reciprocal treatment of debtors, cash restraints can put pressure on relationships with suppliers and lead to other problems if payments are delayed. And so the effective use of cash has to include these other consequences when assessing the appropriate turnover levels to achieve.

The working capital turnover ratio

No catalogue of asset turnover ratios would be complete without explaining the use, and value, of the *working capital ratio*. We have already addressed its components, but it remains to package them into the specific form of this ratio and place it in the context of our model.

Working capital describes that part of a company's assets and liabilities which are being converted into different forms at a significantly faster rate than the rest – somewhat arbitrarily determined as more than once a year. Thus amounts owed to and by the company, its inventories and its cash are regarded as working capital, while long-term funds and the assets which they enable the company to own are not included. Working capital can therefore be defined as an arithmetic formula:

Working capital = Current assets − Current liabilities

Alternatively it can be defined as what is left from equity and long-term liabilities after funding fixed assets:

Working capital =

Shareholders' equity + Long-term liabilities − Fixed assets

In Chapter 3 we recognised the need for long-term funding to cover any long-term working capital requirements and thereby to keep the financial wheels of the enterprise going. Because its components display the common characteristic of short-term liquidity, it can be helpful in summarising the efficiency and effectiveness of those business processes which work together to enable working capital to operate as a whole. And it is therefore helpful to measure the turnover of working capital on the same basis, and alongside its components.

Fixed asset turnover ratios

The *current asset turnover ratio* is a natural concept to understand. Current assets can be traced through the conversion process from raw materials to finished product to cash received from the customer, and round again through purchasing the next batch of raw materials. The turnover ratio for physical assets such as buildings or plant and machinery assets is relatively easy to picture: for instance a piece of machinery turning out product at so many per hour. These are 'tangible assets'.

However a company may include assets on its Balance Sheet such as goodwill which are 'intangible'. It is more difficult to picture the 'turnover' for these assets. And there are many other intangible assets, such as the loyalty of its customers and suppliers and the knowledge and skills of its workforce, which an enterprise would value but does not declare on its balance sheet.

We shall look at these in turn, assess how well the asset turnover ratio (ATR) measures the efficiency, effectiveness and efficacy of these fixed assets and what caveats may apply in using it as the basis for decision-making.

Tangible fixed assets

Firstly, it must be said that the accuracy of any ratio is only as good as the accuracy of its two component parts. There have been many examples of companies taking licence over what they declare as 'revenue' and when they declare it. There are far more choices about how a company values its fixed assets. This is not the place to go into these in detail; suffice it to quote a few examples.

Depreciation and amortisation policies should be disclosed in the notes to the balance sheet. But the sale and leaseback of buildings and other assets may not be. And yet they can dramatically affect the value of assets declared and therefore a firm's turnover ratio. One needs to look no further than the airline industry to see how leasing, rather than purchasing, aircraft can provide 'off-balance-sheet' finance that results in far higher ATRs than would otherwise be the case.

The example of aircraft leasing is well known. However, there are a number of ways that assets can be disguised from the balance sheet and it is as well to understand these in order to achieve a valid assessment of a company's ability to use these assets to generate revenue. Certainly, if the turnover ratio of a company's fixed assets shows a dramatic improvement from one period to the next it would be as well to ask how that has been achieved and whether there has been any significant refinancing or change in accounting treatment.

Having verified, as far as is possible, the accuracy and consistency of the valuation of a company's fixed assets, what is the asset turnover ratio saying about how well they are being managed?

The prime purpose of assets, as illustrated in our model, is to provide capacity and capability. The asset turnover ratio measures this capability in terms of the volume of goods and services that these assets enable the business to sell in the period being reported. This period is normally a year and might be expected to reflect any seasonal fluctuations in the annual cycle. However the ratio performance in that year gives no indication, in isolation, of the capability that is being built within those assets to enable sales in future years.

It is here that trend analysis over a number of years is helpful in assessing how performance is likely to continue. But past performance is no guarantee of the future, and assets can rapidly become obsolete, exhausted, or the victim of external factors. It is therefore important to examine the management policies and practices applied to assets in more detail and consider the environment – physical, political and technological – in which they operate. These factors gain more importance the more critical certain assets are to a business.

Intangible fixed assets

So far we have considered those assets in a company which we can touch and feel – its tangible assets. However, the value of companies and enterprises has become more and more dependent on assets that cannot be touched but can nevertheless be felt – in an intangible way.

These intangible assets usually represent rights that the company or enterprise has acquired which give it the capability to add unique value to the customer. Such rights could be acquired and protected through legal means or they could be acquired and sustained through relationships with various groups of stakeholders.

Patents, copyrights and other forms of intellectual property rights (IPR) are examples of rights acquired through legal means. Reputation and loyalty among customers, suppliers and employees, and what is known as a company's 'licence to operate' in the wider community, are developed over time through the relationships an enterprise establishes and builds with these groups. These means are not mutually exclusive, but one can be used to support the other, for instance where the terms of employee or supplier contracts can help to substitute for areas where mutual trust cannot totally be relied upon.

Tangible assets usually have a discrete purchase price and an estimable useful life. These can be used as the basis for the historical record and ongoing depreciation to arrive at a current valuation which carries the hallmarks of logic and authenticity. And there are some categories of intangible assets for which the accountancy profession has established rules of valuation, for instance forms of IPR referred to above, or the calculation of 'positive goodwill' which specifically arises on the acquisition of another company at a price in excess of that company's value on its balance sheet (its net book value or NBV). But generally it is at this point that accountants are at a loss as to how to value intangible assets. The result is that these assets are mainly absent from the balance sheet valuation of a company (Figure 4.3).

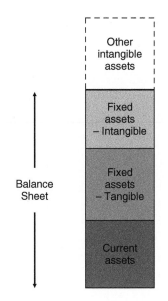

Figure 4.3 Classes of assets

Therefore, while intangible assets can be key in determining the capability of a company to add value and thereby contribute to the revenue side of the equation, they are not included in the value of assets from which the asset turnover ratio is calculated. And we need to look to means other than conventional financial ratios to measure the effectiveness and efficacy with which they are managed.

Questions to ask: The time horizon

There are a number of questions which it is worth considering in assessing the true value of a company's ATR. We would start by asking how critical different forms of assets are to the company. The location of its buildings could be most critical in terms of access to markets or to suppliers with whom close working partnerships may have been developed. The proprietary nature of its research and development facilities may give it a cutting edge in competitive advantage. And the skills and training of its employees may be crucial in providing a unique service to customers. It is helpful to identify which assets are most critical to a firm's success in order to focus on the way those assets are being managed for the long term as well as the short term.

In helping to predict the longer-term viability and success of a business, the next question would be how vulnerable those assets are. We considered the risk to inventory assets of obsolescence. The same can apply to fixed assets which are dependent on old technology, or to employees whose skills could soon be lost in retirement or by other forms of exodus. The brand or reputation of companies can be more or less vulnerable depending on the nature and level of risks in the industry or marketplace in which it operates.

An answer to these questions lies in the strategy that the enterprise is following to cope with these contingent risks. A company that has identified these risks, has plans to address them and is applying those plans is more likely to be able to sustain the potential of its assets. The more flexibility or adaptability it can build into its assets, either by versatility of use for its buildings, length and terms of service for its employees or the ability to upgrade its key plant, the better it will be able to respond to changes in the industry or marketplace. Thus it is important to assess future risk alongside past performance as a measure of the future capability of a firm's assets.

But this is still addressing the short- to medium-term horizon. If the vision for an enterprise provides the strength and depth of inspiration and motivation to create lasting success, it will require assets that can be developed and sustained to provide capability for that success over the long term. Here we are inevitably including the least tangible elements of a company's assets: its very culture and values. These can be seen in the nature of its brand and reputation – the relationship it has with its key stakeholders – and can determine whether any occurrence of those risks referred to above have a temporary or lasting effect.

Responding to key challenges

1. Both tangible and intangible assets, many of which may not appear on the balance sheet, can be critical to a business.
2. We will need to invest time, money and risk in our assets to ensure best use of them.
3. We can assess how efficiently they are used, how effective is their output, and how well they contribute to realising the vision of the business.

And so we return to the key consideration in our model for how assets should be managed so as to realise their full potential – over the long term – to create capacity for an enterprise: that is, the requirements of its various stakeholders. These stakeholders include the employees themselves who represent an essential element of those assets – whether declared on the balance sheet or not. How a firm treats its employees and provides other assets to enable them to develop and realise their skills will determine their willingness to stay with and support the firm through its inevitable ups and downs. The loyalty of customers and suppliers to a firm will be largely influenced by their relationship with its employees. And a firm's 'licence to operate' in a community will be affected by how it treats the environment and respects local laws and customs through the use (or misuse) of its assets.

We shall return to these issues in Chapter 10.

How to maximise value and success

1. Recognise the value of assets not recorded on the balance sheet.
2. Benchmark the productivity of our assets against others in the industry.
3. Balance measures of efficiency in the use of assets with measures of their effectiveness and efficacy.

5

Value add management –
the profit margin

> **Key challenges**
>
> 1. To what extent do our own resources or the markets we serve determine our strategy to add value?
> 2. Where are the potential sources for adding value in the value chain?
> 3. What scope do we have for increasing our profit margin?

Introduction

In the last chapter we focused on the second stage of our business model: how a company manages its resources – its assets – converting the funds available to it into a capacity for adding value. In this chapter we move our attention to the next 'floor', where that capacity is converted into value that is realised, such that the company can take its share – as profit.

Company strategies are sometimes divided into two types: resource-based and market-led. A resource-based strategy focuses on the unique, or at least prevailing, strength of a company's resources, whether it be its people, its technology, its access to raw materials or whatever. Under this strategy the company then seeks to realise the potential of those resources to the full. It is they that provide the competitive edge for the company and enable it to operate more efficiently and effectively than any other.

A market-led strategy, on the other hand, seeks to identify and meet unique requirements, or sets of requirements, in the market place. This is often referred to as *market differentiation* and sets a company apart from its competitors by the particular customer set it is appealing to. To this extent a fully market-led company will employ whatever resources are necessary in order to fully meet the needs of that set of customers.

These two strategies may appear, and are sometimes represented as being, mutually exclusive. It might be tempting to consider resource-based strategies focusing exclusively on the subject of the last chapter, and market-led strategies focusing on the delivery of value add to the customer, which we shall consider here. But in truth they are mutually dependent. Developing unique resources which have no value to the customer, or identifying unique needs which a company does not have the resources to meet, are equally likely to be ineffective in converting resources into value – and thereby profit. Their mutual dependency is illustrated in our model by the prominence given to customer requirements in choosing and developing one's assets, while recognising that assets are key in providing a capacity to add value. But the realisation of that value calls for another level of management altogether.

The profit margin

In our enterprise stewardship model the financial measure of this stage of the business process, expressed as a ratio, is the *profit margin* (Figure 5.1). It seeks to measure the ability of a firm to convert available capacity into actual value. But in doing so it has to take

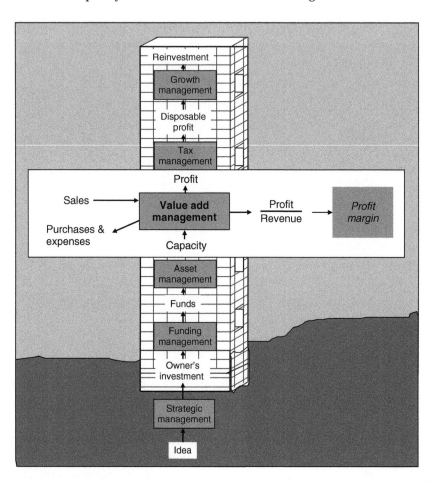

Figure 5.1 Value add management

proper account of the value of what has been consumed. This will include the actual materials and labour used within the product or service, as well as any reduction in future capability caused by their production or delivery.

However, profit itself is a parochial, and somewhat short-sighted, measure of adding value. It measures the process from the point of view of the company itself. It only recognises the immediate value derived from the price that it charges. It does not seek to recognise the value that may be derived by the customer over and above the price paid. And it does not recognise any future value that may be created from its contribution as an investment in the relationship with the customer. The importance of customer loyalty and brand value in achieving sustained success has been given greater credit in recent years.

Managing profit through adding value

The relationship between the value that a company generates and the profit that it calculates and declares is illustrated in Figure 5.2.

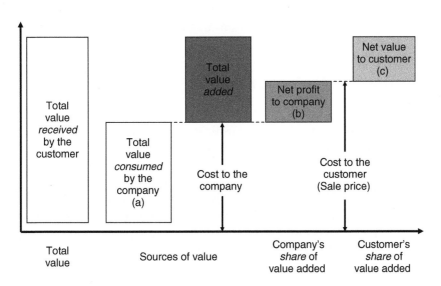

Figure 5.2 The relationship between profit and value added

The total value generated by a company and received by a customer is seen to be made up of three components. The company will have consumed value (a) in converting raw material – and effort – into the product or service which the customer receives. This is calculated as cost to the company and thereby determines the amount of value it has added in total. By setting a selling price for the product or service, the company is determining its own share of that value added (b) – and in a way that provides a financial measure of profit. In the same way the sale price determines the share that the customer receives of the value added (c), although this is rarely as convenient to calculate in financial terms.

This perspective on the process of adding value and the residual role of profit enables an enterprise to align itself to a positive vision of creating value and sustaining success rather than focusing exclusively on profit. Indeed, profit can be a deceptive entity to try to focus on. It seems to perform an illusion whereby it can only be seen when one has one's eyes fixed on the wider context of value and disappears as soon as one tries to direct one's gaze straight at it.

We have described profit as having a residual role in the division of value added. In fact it is only defined in terms of the difference between two other elements: revenue and cost. Even those two elements are not easy to determine independently, but accountants have been more successful at counting cost than at assessing value, so we shall start with examining the relationship of cost to revenue.

Managing the cost margin

As profit is the difference between revenue and cost, one way of increasing a company's profit margin is to reduce costs while maintaining prices. We shall look at the alternative – increasing prices – in the next section.

Our model identifies two sources of cost in the process of managing profit from value add. One comes from using capacity provided by the firm's assets. To the extent that such assets become depleted over time, their replacement must be provided for if the business is to be sustained as a going concern. An allowance is therefore made for 'depreciation' and this is charged against revenue generated during the period. As depreciation is generally related to time rather than usage, it is treated as a 'fixed' cost that has normally to be incurred regardless of volumes. A method is devised, if necessary, to allocate such fixed costs to different products in order to calculate their respective profit margins.

The other source of cost comes from purchases and expenses required in the process of adding value through the products and services provided. These comprise materials, labour and other services bought in. Some of these elements may vary directly with the volume of products and services provided and can be treated as variable costs. However, other elements will not vary in this way. For example, employees represent 'fixed costs' if their salaries and wages are not related to volumes of production or sales.

The traditional way of analysing costs is to distinguish between these fixed and variable costs. Thus the ratio of total cost : revenue can be sub-divided:

Total cost/Revenue =

   Fixed cost / Revenue + Variable cost / Revenue

These separate elements can then be analysed further into their respective components for closer examination.

However, the traditional (or 'resource-based') approach to costing in this way has significant drawbacks in trying to manage cost margins. This is largely due to the difficulty in relating resources directly to products or services. As a result the allocation of these 'fixed costs' to the sale of products and services can be tenuous. A more dynamic and effective approach is that of 'activity-based costing'.

The difference between resource-based and activity-based approaches is illustrated in Figure 5.3.

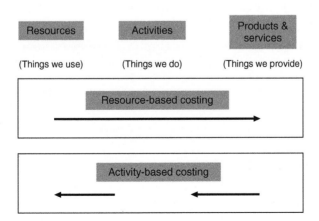

Figure 5.3 Two approaches to cost management

Resource-based costing implies a direct relationship between resources and end-products and seeks to allocate the former to the latter in as fair and equitable a manner as possible. It also implies a direction of causation from 'resources' to 'products', as if the priority is to make best use of resources rather than focus on the products that customers actually require. This is reminiscent of the resource-based strategy we identified earlier.

On the other hand, activity-based costing identifies an intermediary stage and a different direction in the relationship between resources and end-products. It takes a market-led approach and starts with the products and services provided to the customer. It then recognises that products and services require a collection of activities in order to design, produce, market and deliver them – the essence of our value add management process. These activities in turn call for resources to enable them to be carried out. In this way product drives resource rather than the other way round and provides a model for identifying waste and maximising value add.

Managing the profit margin

As we have said, profit itself is an elusive object. It is the company's share of the value it adds to the customer and is dependent on the level of cost it consumes in the process and the price that it sets and receives from the customer.

We have already identified two approaches to cost management which seek to address the drivers of cost in totally different ways. Before we address how pricing affects profit, let us consider how these two approaches can be used in managing profit and introduce a third which addresses profit management from the standpoint of focusing primarily on value (Figure 5.4).

Costing method	Objective	Characteristic	Management focus	Measurement focus
Resource-based	Resource minimisation	Cope with as little resource as possible	Output and productivity	Efficiency
Activity-based	Activity optimisation	Eliminate waste and focus on what adds value	Process and organisation	Effectiveness
Value-based	Value maximisation	Realise as much value as possible from the vision	Marketing and responsiveness	Efficacy

Figure 5.4 Three approaches to profit management

A resource-based approach to profit management seeks to reduce resource costs as much as possible without jeopardising the volume of output. Productivity is the key focus for management and productivity measures abound to help them. These are often expressed as financial ratios in the form of pound's revenue per pound of resource used.

This approach is perhaps most relevant where prices are highly competitive, where the service component of the product is minimal and where quality represents a minimum constraint rather than a source of differentiation. Commodity markets are a good example, where competitive advantage is seen to lie in being most efficient. Certainly the emphasis here is on efficiency, rather than the more subtle objectives of effectiveness or efficacy.

In recent years, frustration has risen with using a resource-based model to address the increasing levels of what is seen as overhead cost (or 'burden') within companies. In addition, the service element has become more and more important within a company's product offering. As a result, 'activities' have been identified as the missing link which enables organisations to unpack and manage this elusive element of cost.

By focusing on the processes which drive activities and then resources in order to deliver products and services, it is possible to distinguish those activities, at any level of detail, which are actually contributing to meeting end-customer requirements, that is adding value, and those which are not. In this way waste can be identified and eliminated and resources better organised to focus on what adds value.

By mapping the value adding process for an enterprise it is therefore possible to analyse the 'fixed cost' margin. This is something which the allocation process within resource-based systems had been notably unable to do. By using activity-based costing it has become feasible to measure how effective even the most 'fixed cost' parts of the organisation are in contributing to profitability.

The activity-based model naturally leads to the third approach to profit management. Value-based management uses the activity-based model but goes further than identifying waste and thereby reducing cost. It looks not only at what is being currently provided to its current market, but at what additional value could be added, not only to its existing customers but to other potential markets. Thus each activity can be examined for its potential efficacy as well as its efficient and effective operation.

Here the management focus is to identify how the product or service (to the extent that they can be distinguished from one another) can be improved and how customer requirements can be anticipated or prompted. As the potential for adding value increases, so the potential for a greater share of that value presents itself through the profit margin.

Pricing for profit

We have considered ways that the profit margin can be analysed and improved through managing costs. However, there are a number of alternative ways in which a company can improve its profit margin. Figure 5.5 illustrates alternative ways to double a profit margin.

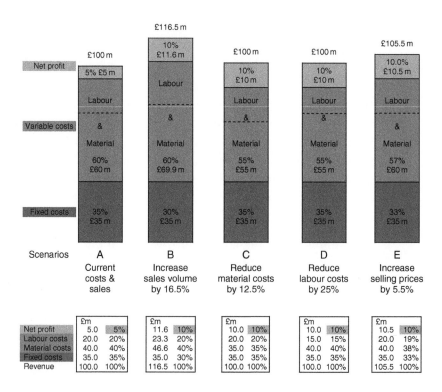

Figure 5.5 Alternative ways of doubling your profit margin

The first **Scenario A** shows the example of a firm earning £5 m profit from a revenue of £100 m in a year – a profit margin of 5 per cent.

This profit is what is left to the company after deducting £60 m of variable costs – material (£40 m) and direct labour (£20 m) – and charging £35 m fixed costs as depreciation for the replacement of fixed assets.

If the company wishes to double its profit margin, it has a number of possible strategies to follow. One option, **Scenario B**, is to try to increase sales from its existing capacity. It would take a 16.5 per cent increase in sales to double the profit margin in this way. This is quite feasible if there is that amount of excess capacity within the company's fixed assets. But, as pointed out earlier, this applies to all 'overhead', not just the assets that are included on the balance sheet, and it may therefore represent a more ambitious target when extended to all support areas of the business.

Another strategy is to reduce material costs while maintaining sales volumes and prices. Efficiencies might be achieved through reduction in waste, redesign or re-sourcing of raw materials or components. However, this would have to amount to a 12.5 per cent reduction in total in order to achieve a 10 per cent profit margin as illustrated in **Scenario C**, without any reduction in value of the product or service requiring a reduction in price.

The other key element of variable costs is direct labour and **Scenario D** shows that it would require a 25 per cent reduction in such costs in order to achieve a commensurate increase in profit margin. Any investment in capital assets would require further savings in order to compensate for the resulting costs of depreciation. Even with the re-design of antiquated production lines into work cells with a multi-skilled workforce, this is a demanding target.

None of these ways of doubling a company's profit margin are impossible under certain circumstances. However, as **Scenario E** demonstrates, an increase in the real or perceived value of a product or service which enables a company to increase its prices by 5.5 per cent achieves the same result: a doubling of its profit margin from 5 per cent to 10 per cent. This point is perhaps self-evident, but it becomes a more attractive proposition when compared with the far more significant step changes required in volumes or costs to achieve the same result.

So how does one go about increasing value? To the extent that 'value is in the eye of the beholder', it may be argued that the most lucrative means of increasing such value is to increase the customer's awareness of it. And so there is a case for marketing and brand management in order to enable the price of a firm's product to more closely reflect such heightened appreciation.

There are also many techniques which enable prices to be increased without being obvious: re-packaging, joint marketing and so on. However, there may be a limit to how far such methods can be exploited in an increasingly sophisticated market. Far more longer lasting is an increase in real value which can be shared with the customer through appropriate pricing. And, as we shall see later in this chapter, a common opportunity for adding value is by reducing cost or wasteful activity for the customer.

And so this is not an argument for inflationary price rises. The scenario here is based on a real increase in value for the customer, achieved through the process of value analysis and improvement referred to above, in the same way as firms have traditionally addressed cost analysis and reduction. And it does not exclude a combination of the above strategies. It is by reviewing the real value that an enterprise envisages providing, in the most efficient and effective way, that it can develop strategies to achieve it in the most efficacious way. The profit margin is one indicator of the degree to which it is successful in adding value and, as we have seen, it can be influenced by a number of factors in the process of value add management.

The profit margin in the value chain

As we noted earlier the value added by an enterprise, of which profit is the share retained by it, is usually one step in a process of adding value which extends backwards through the supplier and forwards through the customer. It can therefore be helpful to examine how value is added – or lost – in these other steps. In this way further opportunities may come to light in which any one of the enterprises in the 'chain' can reduce cost or add further value over the entire process. If there is such scope, then there is equally scope for another enterprise in the chain to acquire a share of that extra value for its own benefit.

Figure 5.6 illustrates how the value chain provides the key link between companies in converting raw materials into finished goods

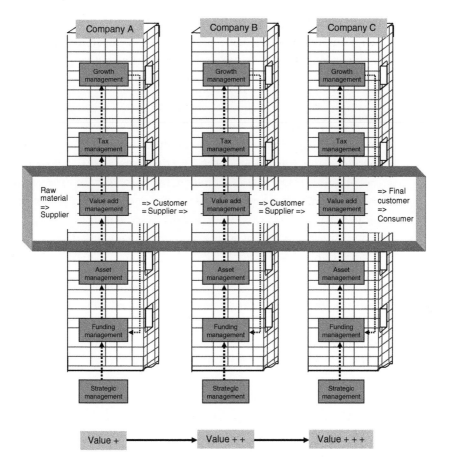

Figure 5.6 The enterprise value chain

or services for ultimate consumption. The example shows three companies involved. There may be many more in a particular chain, and it is often difficult to determine where the chain actually begins or finishes. However, it is helpful for any company to identify the chain as far backwards or forwards as it can see its product or service having a significant influence on value achieved – or perceived. The minutest component can have a critical role in the function of an end product while its perceived value may be at another level altogether.

Managing value

We have identified some possible sources of adding value within the value chain. These cover reducing waste or contributing to functionality and benefit either within the enterprise's own scope or elsewhere. How each company determines its share of that value is down to negotiation. How and with whom that negotiation is conducted (even with the end customer through market testing) will determine the respective shares of profit resulting from the price agreed.

Over and above the value generated by each transaction, and therefore the immediate profit arising, there will be an effect on the ongoing relationship between the two parties. This effect has been recognised in terms of the loyalty of customers and their future propensity to buy. Customer loyalty has been a key feature in the promotion of customer relationship management (CRM) as a management and systems tool.

The benefit for companies in also developing long-term 'partnership' relationships with suppliers, rather than adversarial ones characterised by bartering, has been shown to provide long-term benefits for both parties. While it is important to keep a watchful eye on competition and identify potential substitutes in the market for one's own offering, it is essential for a company to keep its main focus on its customers. By meeting and anticipating its customers' requirements with the unique set of resources at its disposal, it will inevitably be doing its best to compete with others who have responded to the same or similar need but in their own way.

Responding to key challenges

1. Depending on the unique strengths of our resources or our response to unique requirements of our customers, we can adopt resource-based or market-led strategies or a combination of both.
2. Value can be added and derived at any and every point in the value (or supply) chain. It is shared amongst suppliers and customers through the pricing mechanism.
3. The profit margin can be increased by increasing sales, reducing costs or increasing the value we add at less additional cost.

In exploring the drivers of the profit margin we have examined the process by which value is added. Three approaches to profit management have been identified: resource-based, activity-based and value-based. These focus on each of the 'Three Effs' which financial ratios seek to measure: efficiency, effectiveness and efficacy. And we have seen how the ability of an enterprise to add value – and thereby determine its profitability – is intricately linked to other enterprises in the value chain. We shall examine these relationships more closely in Chapter 10.

How to maximise value and success

1. Be clear about what differentiates us in terms of resources, processes or products and services in adding value.
2. Adopt an appropriate method of linking value consumed (costs) with value generated (revenue).
3. Explore opportunities to add value over the entire value chain.

Tax management – the effective tax rate

Note – Where specific examples are given of tax and accounting treatment, particularly in this chapter, these are based on regulations in the UK.

Introduction

We pick up the story in our model at the point where an enterprise has acquired a profit (or a loss) as its share of the value it has added for (or deducted from) the customer. We will now consider how that profit is to be used or distributed to those stakeholders who have a claim to it.

We say 'stakeholders' rather than 'shareholders' because the first call on a company's profits is from a diverse group of stakeholders represented by the government through the Inland Revenue. As we shall see in Chapter 10 the wider community have an interest and a contribution to make in enabling enterprises to succeed. Its contribution is in providing an environment and infrastructure that enable a firm to operate. These range from security – law and order – to health and education for its employees. While the government has a number of sources of funding – including taxation of employees through PAYE and sales through VAT – it makes a claim on the profits of companies as one of those sources.

This is not the first time that the company's activities have contributed directly to funding community requirements. As mentioned above, companies provide indirect funding to the exchequer through the income tax (PAYE) that employees pay from their salaries and wages. This is a tax on that share of the value added by a company that is given to the employees who have contributed to it. Value Added Tax (VAT) is, strictly speaking, a tax on the customer (or rather the ultimate consumer), levied as an uplift to the sales price a company charges. In this sense income tax and corporation tax are taxes on *value added* by suppliers whereas VAT is a tax on *value received* by the ultimate consumer. Therein lies the distinction between direct and indirect methods of taxation.

Management and administration

As well as the need to *manage* the process of how they are taxed on their profit, companies are more and more being required to *administer* other processes of taxation as well. We shall not address this here but it is important that companies have efficient processes that comply with the law for dealing with the administration of PAYE, VAT and the increasing requirements of benefits such as child and working tax credits and so on.

The process we are addressing here is that of managing the tax that is due to the government from the value that an enterprise has added – through income tax for unincorporated businesses or corporation tax for those that are incorporated. Charities, of course, have a special status. On the grounds that they are in existence to benefit the community in some way, they are not required to make a separate contribution through taxation.

So what is there to manage? Is there not a clear statement of the profits declared by a company in its annual accounts and, in most cases, a requirement for such accounts to be professionally audited? And is there not a simple rate of Corporation Tax to be applied to most companies, with concessionary rates for companies just starting out or for those earning low levels of profit? Surely one simply multiplies one by the other to compute the share due to the government.

Two types of profit

Well, it doesn't necessarily work exactly like that. The profits that are derived from a company's trading activities for use in reporting to shareholders and the outside world are generated on a number of commercial principles. These are set out by the Accounting Standards bodies and allow for some discretion in arriving at a 'true and fair view' of a company's activities and, in particular, its profit. This derives from the desire to quantify, as closely as possible, the 'true' value that a company has added in a period and retained for itself.

For the sake of equity and justice, the government seeks to apply the same rules across all enterprises. And so it has introduced over the years a body of legislation, often supplemented by a Finance Act at least once a year, which defines exactly how profits are to be computed for tax purposes.

As a result, the amount shown as profit in the annual accounts is not usually the same amount of profit that is assessed for tax purposes and, in nearly every case, it is necessary to make adjustments from one to the other as required by the Taxes Acts and other provisions. Therefore, as our model illustrates (Figure 6.1) the amount of profit left after tax has been deducted (NAT), as a proportion of profit before such deductions (NBT) can reflect an 'effective' after-tax profit rate different from the standard rate.

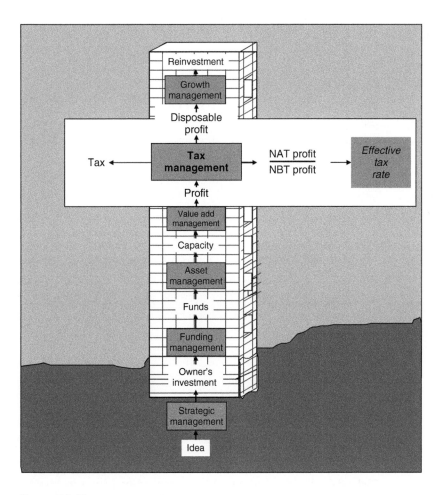

Figure 6.1 Tax management

It is important that directors – both executive and non-executive – and other officials and interested parties are able to understand the reasons for variation. By doing so they will be able to anticipate where such variations may reverse themselves during some future period of reporting. It will also help them identify any potential fraud or misrepresentation where significant differences persist.

Different rules

'Adjustments' can arise from a number of sources. This is not the place to go into the technical details. However, the main cause is the application of rules for charging against profits the use of fixed assets in a business.

Most companies apply a 'straight-line' method of depreciating assets such as their plant and machinery used for manufacturing or delivering their product or service over a standard number of years, say five. However, the Inland Revenue applies a system of *capital allowances* which typically allow 25 per cent of an asset's value to be 'written down' against profits each year. This is done on a 'rolling' basis, so that each year 25 per cent is applied to whatever is left from the previous year. Inevitably this produces differences in the amounts charged against profits for taxation or accounting purposes. In this way it provides probably the most common reason for divergences between profits reported in the accounts and those on which tax is calculated.

The Taxes Acts also provides exceptions to the rule of '25 per cent writing down allowance'. The government has, at various times, introduced incentives for investment in particular geographical areas, industries or types of activity within companies. As a result there are provisions for accelerating allowances by increasing the charges in the first year.

Over the years governments have identified areas to encourage investment, calling them variously 'special development areas' or 'enterprise zones'. These have been designed to attract investment by allowing companies to charge the cost of it against taxable profits earlier than they would otherwise do so on a commercial basis.

In the past governments have sought to encourage the use of information technology by enabling small enterprises to write off such investment in full in the first year as if it were an expense. In a similar way, there are special provisions to encourage investment in research and development.

Finally, as a wider incentive for the growth of new enterprises, central government has introduced a higher rate of allowance across the board for small- and medium-size enterprises (known as SMEs) in the first year of any qualifying investment.

There are a number of other reasons for 'adjustments', for instance as a result of the treatment of losses or provisions for bad debts. This list is not exhaustive but provides examples of reasons why such 'adjustments' have to be made to profits computed on sound commercial principles in order to comply with the rules used for assessing the amount of tax to pay in a given year. They may provide clues as to why the 'effective tax rate' for any company may differ from that which would result from the appropriate rate applied to the profits declared in the annual accounts. And they may provide the source of questions as to whether the company has taken full advantage of such incentives in managing its operations to be most tax efficient.

Common principles

However, the most valuable commodity to apply in achieving the most effective tax rate – or in challenging it – is common sense. This is embodied in four fundamental accounting principles or 'concepts' that the accounting bodies have set out. They seek to apply these in setting hard-and-fast rules and regulations as well as in deriving a 'true and fair view' of a company's financial statements.

The first principle is the *going concern concept.* This is to assume that a business will continue to operate for the foreseeable future. In the context of tax management, it provides a good reminder that it is the sustained success of the enterprise that should be at the heart of every decision. The temptation to reduce the tax bill in the short term by doing things which are not in its long-term interests should be resisted.

The second principle flows from the first in that it seeks to accurately assess the ongoing operations of a firm. The *accruals concept* recognises that cash flow does not necessarily reflect the flow of value add and allows for such adjustments as may be necessary to recognise income as it is actually earned and costs as they are genuinely incurred.

The third principle is that of *consistency* and also follows logically from the first principle. It requires that the same accounting treatment is applied to similar items and activities during each period and from one period to another.

Finally an overriding principle of *prudence* is applied in order only to recognise profits when they are realised and not to anticipate them before value has been earned and the company's share reasonably secured.

Avoidance, evasion and making the best of it

The process of tax management is about arranging the operations of an enterprise to benefit from incentives and allowances offered by the government on behalf of the wider community, while ensuring that any actions taken to benefit from such incentives are in line with the long term interests and vision of the enterprise. These actions can achieve an avoidance of tax without evading it, but it is the role of everyone involved in this process to ensure that the distinction is clear and that the risks of evasion and fraud are avoided. In this way a genuine contribution can be made to the community through the tax paid. It is perhaps surprising that companies often appear embarrassed about the level of tax they pay.

Certainly shareholders may view it as a direct reduction in the amount available to them. But companies might equally express the tax they pay in terms of the direct benefit they receive from public expenditure in providing them with an environment and external infrastructure in which to operate. More specifically, a company might see such benefits as contributing to its wider, longer-term vision as an enterprise.

A company in the health care sector might express the tax it pays each year in terms of its contribution to the provision of hospital and other facilities which work together with its own products or services to benefit people's health and lifestyle – similarly for companies in the food, leisure and even entertainment industries. With a little imagination, each company's 'tax burden' could be seen as a further way in which it contributes value to those who also participate in its enterprise as customers, suppliers, employees, shareholders or members of the wider community.

Responding to key challenges

1. There are different rules which affect the calculation and timing of profits declared for taxation and reporting.
2. There are four main principles underlying the compilation of company accounts: going concern, accruals, consistency and prudence.
3. Tax avoidance is the organisation of a taxpayer's affairs so that the minimum tax liability is incurred, whereas tax evasion is the minimisation of tax liability by illegal means.

How to maximise value and success

1. Take advantage of tax incentives where doing so supports the strategic objectives of the business.
2. Treat tax paid by the business as sharing value with the community and a mark of success.
3. Avoid tax without evading it.

Growth management – the payout and retention ratios

Key challenges

1. How can a business best use its profits?
2. How do we evaluate the case for investment?
3. What are the sources of growth for a business?

Introduction

In the last chapter we examined one application of the profit earned by a company, through the payment of tax due to the Inland Revenue. This is a statutory duty, just as it is for us as individuals to pay income tax on what we earn. Once we have dispensed such obligation as individuals we are left with disposable income. Companies are left with the equivalent – disposable profit, referred to as net after-tax (NAT) profit.

What a company does with its disposable profit is largely at its own discretion. However, there may be obligations it has to its 'preference' shareholders to distribute dividends to them before being able to consider paying dividends to holders of 'ordinary' shares. Dividends to preference shareholders are based on a fixed percentage of the nominal value of the shares they hold (e.g. 5 per cent preference shares). If the company has not earned profits in previous years to be able to pay such dividends, it may be obliged to 'catch up' with any arrears when profits allow if the preference shares it issued included this condition (e.g. 5 per cent cumulative preference shares).

The distribution of profits – a simple decision?

There is a simple choice facing a company in the application of its disposable profit: to distribute it or to retain it. The mechanism for distributing profit is by issuing dividends to its shareholders. Any undistributed profit becomes available for reinvestment or future distribution. The proportion of NAT profit that is distributed as dividends, as illustrated in our model, is known as the *payout ratio*. The proportion that is retained within the company is known as the *retention ratio* (Figure 7.1).

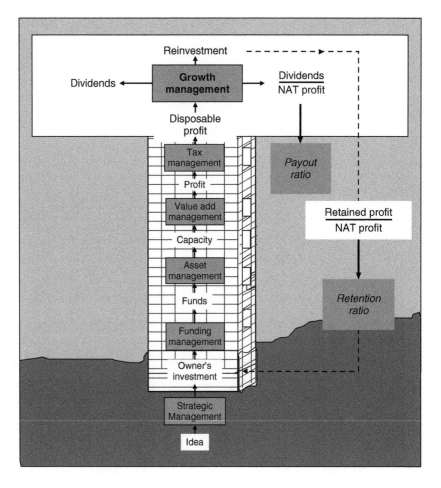

Figure 7.1 Growth management

So is this not a simple decision? And why is this process in our model called 'growth management'? In this chapter we shall explore the considerations required in making this 'simple' decision and why it can be crucial in determining the opportunity and direction for the growth of the enterprise. These considerations will be viewed from two perspectives. The first is from the point of view of the shareholder receiving the dividend pay out. The second is from the company's point of view as it seeks to grow and provide for the future. While the process might appear to involve simply a 'division of the spoils', we shall see that, if taken judiciously, the decision can serve the interests of both the shareholders and the company as a whole.

The shareholder's perspective – a return on investment?

Shareholders are the legal owners of a company. As such they can have a dual interest in the enterprise, not only as an investment but also as a vehicle for realising its purpose – the original vision that the founders had for it, or that which has been developed and adapted by those subsequently leading it.

Most shareholders view their interest simply as investors and as such are only interested in their 'return' on that investment. A return can be realised as income through receiving dividends or as a capital gain if they sell their shares at a higher price than when they bought them.

The components of shareholder value

The income that shareholders receive through dividends is largely determined by the level of profits being earned by the company. However, the change in value of their shares can be far less reliable or predictable, being influenced as much by what is happening in the industry and economy as anything the company may determine.

Much has been written and devised in an attempt to rationalise the market valuation of a company's shares. That is beyond the scope of this book. In theory any profit retained within the company should be reflected in an increase in the value of its assets. Indeed the balance sheet requires this as part of its 'balancing' logic when retained profits are added to reserves.

But this accounting logic does not dictate valuation by market forces. Share values can move independently of the values of assets recorded in a company's books. Other forces are invariably at work to upset the relationship. There is also a strong argument for valuing shares on the basis of the *future* potential of a company rather than its current or past record in earning profits. In recent years many attempts have been made to identify the components of 'shareholder value' within a company and how it influences share prices.

A critical consideration from the shareholders' point of view is whether the business can put profits retained within the business to a more effective use than the shareholders could themselves, either by re-investing its dividends in other companies or using the income for their own consumption.

These alternatives involve varying levels of risk and personal preference. Theorists seek to quantify them by establishing 'hurdle rates' of return required by companies to satisfy shareholders. Techniques of appraisal such as 'economic value add' and 'market value add' apply these hurdle rates as the cost of capital which a company must achieve before it can exceed its shareholders' requirements. If it can, then this should lead to increased demand – and a higher price – for its shares.

The company's perspective – a vehicle for growth

If a company merely puts whatever profit it does not distribute as dividends into its reserves and does not make good use of the equivalent cash, it may be adding to its assets but not to its potential. Retained profits are an opportunity for growth and it is important that, in making the decision as to how much of its profits to distribute, a company has a clear view of its potential use for such profits within the business.

Some of the elements within this process are explored further in Chapter 9 on strategic management, but for now it is helpful to distinguish two methods of growth for a company: organically or by acquisition. There are hybrid versions of these, for instance through partnerships or joint ventures, but whatever strategy a company is following will place demands on its ability to provide funds internally for investment or to raise capital in the open market.

The case for growth

Before we continue with the question of how growth might be financed, we need to establish the case for growth and how its benefits can be evaluated. As mentioned earlier, a company's value is established as much by its future potential as by its past record or by the current 'street' value of its assets. But how does one assess the demand for growth, however financed, generated by the future potential of an enterprise?

Cash flows

The conventional approach to investment appraisal is to attempt to reduce the benefits arising from an investment to the crude level of cash flows. There are three main models which are employed to determine whether an investment is worth making or how to choose between competing demands for limited investment funds. They are illustrated in Figure 7.2 and explained below.

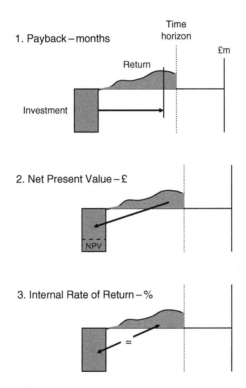

Figure 7.2 Techniques of investment appraisal

The simplest model (1) calculates the amount of time anticipated for the surplus cash flows generated by an investment to recover its original cost. This is known as the *payback* method. A second, more sophisticated model (2), applies a discount factor to future cash flows. In this way it seeks to give these future flows a *net present value.* This can then be compared to the initial outflow required from the investment. The discount factor to be applied can be based on the cost of financing, the degree of risk and other factors. The third method (3) involves applying a specific *internal rate of return* which can be calculated and which produces a net present value of zero.

Whichever technique is applied, the challenge still remains to reduce the anticipated future benefits of an investment to the crude level of cash flow. This approach is consistent with a resource-based strategy for growth which seeks to maximise the efficient use of resources – in this case cash. However it is particularly vulnerable to the risk of changes in assumptions and to the uncertainty of outcome. This is something which can only be accommodated crudely by the use of the 'discount factor' applied in the appraisal formula.

Profit flows

The conventional 'cash flow' approach to investment appraisal seeks to protect the long-term liquidity of an enterprise by ensuring that funds are increased or at least replenished over time. This is a critical need, as companies go bankrupt not through making losses but through running out of cash. However, if a company is seeking not only to be a 'going concern' but to grow and realise the potential of its vision, it should look more to the profit it is generating rather than necessarily the extent to which that is realised in cash. When a company distributes dividends to its shareholders the amount it retains is expressed in terms of profit rather than cash and it is this that provides the source for reinvestment from internal funds.

It may be more appropriate therefore to assess the demand for retained profits in terms of the profitability of potential investment projects rather than simply the cash flows arising from them. This approach recognises benefits that do not necessarily manifest themselves in cash flows within the appraisal period (although it might be argued that ultimately all profit must be realised in cash). It is more aligned to measuring how effective an investment is in the benefit it produces for the company rather than simply how efficient it is in the use of its cash resources.

Value flows

Profit, as we have seen, is only a portion of the value that an enterprise generates. It ignores that part that the customer receives over and above the price they pay. In the same way other contributors to the enterprise – employees and suppliers in particular – will be receiving a benefit over and above the payments they receive. This helps to secure their continued support and loyalty.

Thus if a company is to choose those investments which contribute most to the long-term realisation of its potential – its vision – it is important that it takes regard not only of intangible benefits that may not readily manifest themselves in cash flows for the company but also of benefits that accrue elsewhere. These are benefits that are received by groups who may be outside the company's legal boundaries but who nevertheless form an integral part of its wider 'enterprise' and ultimately determine its future success.

In this way the company is assessing the most efficacious outcome for all and can anticipate receiving an appropriate share of that over-all benefit in the future. The shareholders will then be fulfilling their dual role. They will be both receiving an appropriate return over time as investors and exercising their appropriate roles as owners and stewards of the enterprise.

The options for growth

When deciding how much to distribute and how much to retain from disposable profits, it is important to recognise the respective needs of shareholders and other participants in the enterprise – as set out above. If the focus for the decision is the potential for growth, then the best opportunity for reconciling such needs over time is by maximising the size of the cake, rather than being preoccupied with how it is sliced up.

A secondary consideration is the method by which growth is to be achieved. There are a number of alternatives depending on the objectives and circumstances of the growth opportunity.

The natural source of funding for organic growth is through rein-vested funds. If growth is by diversification, the risk and opportunity posed by such growth may call for the issue of new equity on the market. If it is to be by acquisition, the offer of equity to the share-holders of the target company may be more appropriate. If growth is to be by significant investment in assets in existing lines of busi-ness, borrowing through the issue of bonds could match the low-risk return which they are expected to generate. Finally, a combination of these factors may make the issue of hybrid instruments such as convertible bonds an appropriate source of finance whereby the benefits of an initial fixed-interest return can be combined with a subsequent option to convert to equity at a certain price.

The sources of growth

We can identify the alternative sources of financing in the top 'floor' of our model (see Figure 7.1). That portion of disposable profit which a company retains – its retention ratio – provides an immediate source of internal funding. That portion which it distributes as dividend – its payout ratio – provides, through the return demonstrated to existing shareholders, the basis for future external funding from the issue of new equity. Finally, the level of risk – and confidence – carried by current shareholders influences the extent of 'gearing' that can be achieved in raising borrowings as an alternative to share capital. This was covered in Chapter 3 when we examined the gearing ratio under the funding management process.

And so our model illustrates this ongoing provision of funding – and ongoing creation of value. It can be used to track the generation of value through an enterprise and how that value is realised and distributed amongst the various participants. At each stage in the process the efficiency, effectiveness and efficacy of the enterprise can be measured. However, as our definition of success becomes more sophisticated, the currency of money and the arithmetic of ratios become ever cruder tools to use. They can be helpful guides but dangerous masters and should be used with appropriate discretion and understanding.

Responding to key challenges

1. A business can either distribute or reinvest its profits. How it decides will determine its opportunity to fund growth in the future.
2. Investment can be evaluated on the basis of how it contributes to future cash or profit flows, or the realisation of the underlying vision of the enterprise.
3. A business can grow organically or by acquisition and can fund that growth internally through reinvestment of profits or externally through additional borrowing or equity.

How to maximise value and success

1. Determine the opportunities for the business to grow.
2. Compare the risks of investment with the rewards expected from those risks.
3. Understand the requirements and preferences of existing and potential shareholders and lenders for dividends, interest payments or share growth.

PART THREE
Using Financial Ratios

The composite ratios

> ### Key challenges
>
> 1. How can I compare my business with others?
> 2. How can I measure the performance of a business at an overall level?
> 3. What other measures could be useful at a more detailed level?

Introduction

Over the last five chapters we have been examining the key processes that management engage in to develop their business. Few managers may follow these processes consciously in accordance with this model. But, as we have seen, the model traces the key steps that they will inevitably be taking in managing a business from within. It then maps upon these processes the key ratios used in applying a financial assessment from outside.

Financial ratios do not tell the full story of an enterprise. Nor do they prescribe the course of action to take in any of the key areas of decision-making. They are at best a crude representation, in financial terms, of the performance of an enterprise in its key processes. Achieving the optimum combination of share price and dividend yield for its shareholders may be the sole measure of success that a company chooses. But, where a company recognises the contribution from, and thereby due to, other participants in the enterprise and seeks to do so over the long-term, its management should look to other indicators, financial and otherwise, to measure its true and sustainable success.

Our model provides a framework for describing a business in financial terms and is particularly useful for viewing it from the perspective of the investor/shareholder. However, different companies will see success in different terms. They may therefore be aiming for different destinations and have different journeys for getting there. In a play on the well-known phrase, there will be different courses for different horses. While it can be useful to compare the journey one business is taking against another, it is important to bear in mind that each business may have a different destination and its optimum journey may be unique based on its particular visions and values and tailored to its particular circumstances and resources. Therefore, while it can be helpful to use points of reference – or benchmarks – to learn from others, it is important to recognise that they should be treated as guides for direction rather than necessarily as targets to aim for.

Benchmarking – risks and opportunities

If a business is seeking to maximise long-term value and success it is helpful to have both a target to aim for and reference points to compare progress. It is also useful to measure performance against

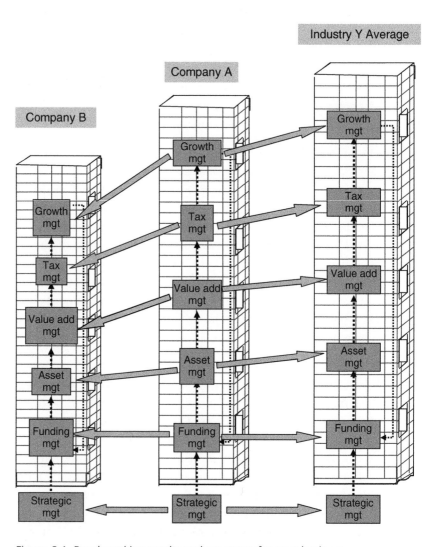

Figure 8.1 Benchmarking results and processes for your business

the industry as a whole as well as selected companies, perhaps its key competitor(s). Figure 8.1 illustrates the way the Enterprise Stewardship Model can be used to benchmark a company (A) against a competitor (B) or the average results in the industry (Y).

Appendix 3 gives an example of benchmarking a business against a competitor. The CD-ROM which accompanies this book also provides an opportunity to record and present a benchmarking exercise for your own company. The data required to calculate the ratios are publicly available from accounts filed at Companies House. Many companies include them in full or summary form on their web sites and there are a number of services available by searching the internet which provide ratios for selected industries, albeit for a fee. The *Almanac of Business and Industrial Financial Ratios* (see Further Reading) is a useful encyclopaedia of statistics for this purpose.

Measuring performance is one aspect of benchmarking, known as *results benchmarking*. It can help management see where their business stands in relation to others and what the performance gap is in different areas. However it does not necessarily help point to how those differences arise and what can be done to address them if desired. Managers require an understanding and comparison of the processes used by different companies in achieving those results. This other discipline of benchmarking is known as *process benchmarking* and should be used alongside the comparison of results. In this way managers can identify what changes may be required in the way that the business operates, in order to achieve the desired results.

The Enterprise Stewardship Model provides a valuable framework to apply both these disciplines. In the first case, financial ratios measuring the five key process stages for a business can be compared to those achieved by the average of all businesses in that industry or to selected competitors. Differences can then be examined to understand how the industry or specific companies manage each step in the process to achieve their results. Companies will vary in size and shape to one another and represent different proportions to the industry as a whole. Financial ratios eliminate differences in size by measuring relative inputs and outputs. But the model helps to illustrate differences in shape resulting from different profiles of results at different floors in the building.

It is very tempting to use financial ratios to 'benchmark' firms against one another. For potential investor-shareholders this may be considered a sufficient guide as to where to invest, but caution must accompany their use, particularly where these measures are used at a summary, or composite, level.

Summarising performance – the composite financial ratios

We shall now revisit these summary ratios that are used in financial evaluation of companies, particularly by investor-shareholders, and which are often used to compare the performance of companies across an industry and even between industries. We have explained in Chapter 2 how these composite ratios are derived. We shall now explore how they can best be used.

The return on assets ratio

The *return on assets* (ROA) ratio (Figure 8.2) embraces the core operational processes within an enterprise. It extends from the creation of physical value, through the management of its assets, to the production and delivery of value to the customer. As we can see, it comprises the profit margin and asset turnover ratio and these can combine in a variety of ways to produce the same result. Thus a low asset turnover ratio combined with a high profit margin can produce the same return on assets as a high asset turnover ratio and low-profit margin.

These patterns can be characteristic of different industries or different segments within an industry. A commonly used illustration is that of a jeweller and a supermarket. A jeweller's shop typically has a high profit margin but low turnover of stock while a supermarket will have a high stock turnover on relatively low profit margin items. These two types of business represent opposite extremes of asset turnover rate and profit margin but can achieve comparable returns on their assets. Thus benchmarking at this level can be a useful indicator but must be used with great caution if the respective dynamics of the enterprises being compared are not fully understood.

The return on equity ratio

The *return on equity* (ROE) ratio presents a broader measure than the return on capital assets ratio. It was calculated in Chapter 2

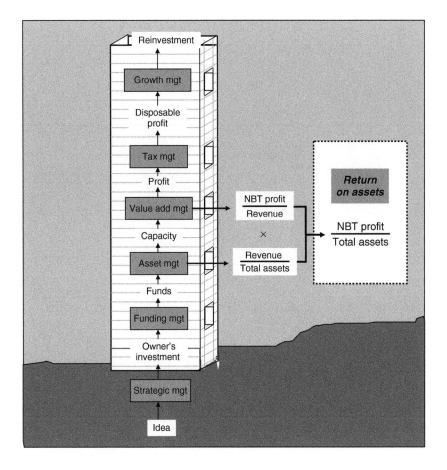

Figure 8.2 The return on assets ratio

and is illustrated again here in Figure 8.3. By extending its scope to include funding management and tax management, it specifically addresses the interests of the shareholder who has invested money in the enterprise and wants to know how the company has affected that investment. It is also of interest to potential investors who wish to consider a company's past performance in stewarding other share-holders' money before deciding on an investment themselves.

The fact that the ROE ratio incorporates the ROA ratio means that the same caveats apply in regard to benchmarking. In addition, the inclusion of funding management and tax management processes requires understanding of the dynamics involved in those areas for any one company before an informed judgement can be made.

There can be significant variations in the effective tax rates that companies pay (and therefore the proportion of profit available to the

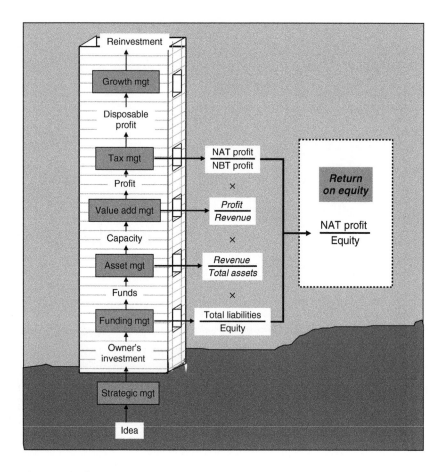

Figure 8.3 The return on equity ratio

shareholders after tax). However, these are likely to be a relatively minor consideration for shareholders compared to the variations in levels of gearing by different companies and their attendant blends of risks and rewards. As we saw in Chapter 3, equity is only one source of long-term funding. The level of commitment to pay interest on borrowings is a major determinant of the level – and likelihood – of return to the shareholders.

The dividend yield

The ROE in a company measures the amount of profit at the disposal of management for the benefit of the shareholders. Although this profit is 'disposable', not all of it is disposed of through distribution as dividends. There is always an element of risk associated with equity investment and many shareholders and investment

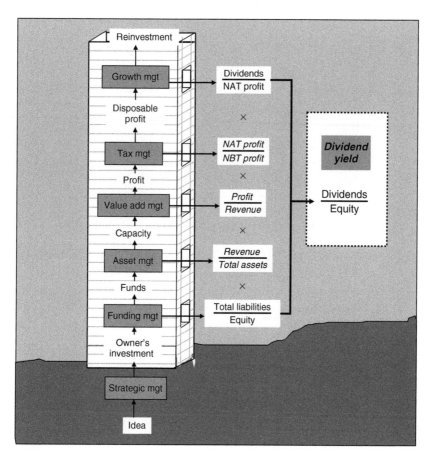

Figure 8.4 The dividend yield

funds require an income from their investment rather than rely on fluctuations in share values. For this reason the amount of profit actually distributed through dividends assumes key importance. The *dividend yield* specifically measures the cash income generated for shareholders from the book value of their investment (Figure 8.4).

On the other hand, shareholders may prefer the prospect of capital gains in the value of their shareholdings. In this case the payout ratio will still be of interest, but as an indicator of the growth potential that the company is sacrificing through distributing profits rather than reinvesting them. However, provided this strategy supports the option of raising new capital as a result of the dividend income it would offer, it may still be in these shareholders' interests.

Of course if a shareholder has purchased shares on the open market or at any value other than the 'nominal' one at which the company holds them in its balance sheet, then the real return will depend on the price which the shareholder actually paid.

In the same way, prospective investors might look to the current market price and the company's track record to assess what actual yield they might expect from buying shares in that company. However, past performance or policy is no guarantee – except for cumulative preference shareholders – of future income. And so the dividend yield measure extends the element of risk and uncertainty contained within the ROE measure.

Profit, dividends and market prices

We have already referred to the alternative ways of measuring dividend income. This can be in relation to the nominal value of shares, as our model illustrates, or in relation to the investment made by a shareholder purchasing shares at market prices. In the latter case the dividend yield is a more relevant measure for the shareholder than using historical and therefore, to the shareholder, arbitrary values. An alternative way of measuring the dividend stream is in terms of dividends per share (DPS). This may be helpful in assessing the trend of dividend payouts without distorting it with variations in share prices. However any new share issues, particularly rights issues or bonus issues, should be factored in to avoid artificial distortions.

Another way of assessing trends in profits available to shareholders in a particular company is to measure the flow of profits per share. In this case the term 'earnings' is given to after-tax profits and the term used for this ratio is *earnings per share* (EPS).

Finally, just as dividend performance can be measured as dividend yield against nominal values, as in our model, or market values, so earnings can also be measured against the market value of shares and expressed as an earnings yield. This provides a more relevant measure for the investor than the company, since a company holds shares in its accounts at a constant nominal value – in accordance with the 'going concern' principle.

Other variations on a theme

We have identified three core composite ratios, ROA, ROE and dividend yield, as being helpful in assessing the performance of companies, especially from a shareholder's perspective. As our model

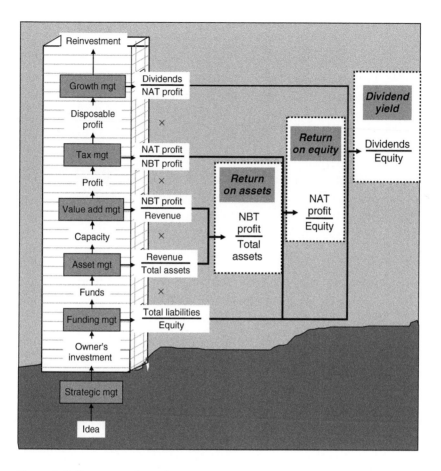

Figure 8.5 The composite ratios

illustrates (Figure 8.5), these provide an ever widening scope of measurement spreading out from the core activity of any enterprise: its ability to produce and deliver value to its customers. So are there other measures that can be derived from the building blocks of our model and used to support the management of a business to success?

Certainly other measures could be derived. But they do not carry the relevance and application of the ones we have selected. From a shareholder's perspective, it is important to measure the profit and dividends generated from a shareholding. It is hardly meaningful to seek to identify, for example, the level of revenue attributable to shareholders or the level of profit attributable to them before the Inland Revenue has been given its share.

Conclusion

In the Introduction we set out three aspects of business that it is important to assess: its efficiency, its effectiveness and its efficacy. *Efficiency* is most relevant to the way an enterprise manages its assets and generates value from them. The asset turnover ratio and to a lesser extent the profit margin are therefore the best indicators of efficiency and these combine together in the return on assets ratio.

We have seen that the return on equity and the dividend yield can be helpful shorthand ratios for shareholders to use in assessing the *effectiveness* with which a company uses their investment. However they can only seek to represent financial compensation for the qualitative elements of risk involved.

But none of these financial ratios can do justice to the quintessential elements of a business enterprise. They fall short of measuring the *efficacy* of how its operations fulfil the true purpose of that enterprise. They only come close if that purpose is confined to quantitative targets expressed in financial terms.

Responding to key challenges

1. Benchmarking can be used to compare the performance and processes of one business with another or with its industry.
2. Composite ratios can be used to measure the performance of a business at summary levels which encompass more than one key process within it.
3. Financial ratios can be analysed into component parts to measure and compare detailed elements of a business' key processes.

We shall need to delve beneath the surface of our model to explore the hidden depths of an enterprise which may have other criteria and purposes than simply to generate profits for its shareholders and other financial benefits for employees, suppliers and customers alike. In doing so we shall explore how financial ratios can be used in the strategic management of a company.

How to maximise value and success

1. Take perceptions and expectations into account when using measures based on market values.
2. Distinguish between efficiency, effectiveness and efficacy when interpreting ratios: trends and comparisons.
3. When comparing results against other companies, compare their processes at the same time.

The place of financial ratios
in strategic management

Key challenges

1. What are the main components of strategic management?
2. How do the components of strategic management relate to the main steps in the business process?
3. How can the link be made between strategy and financial performance?

Introduction

In the previous chapters we have explored how an enterprise works – or at least that part of it which is easily visible and measurable. In the context of our model we have examined the use of financial ratios to measure the performance of processes 'above the ground'. We have seen that they make a good attempt to measure the *efficiency* with which an enterprise manages those processes. These ratios are cruder indicators of how *effectively* some of those processes are managed. But they are crudest at measuring how effectively they have been managed in achieving the purpose intended – their *efficacy*.

We have also seen how financial ratios can be helpful in measuring past performance, where money has changed hands in the process of creating and exchanging value. They are likely to be less helpful in assessing future potential, where value has not yet been crystallised in financial terms.

So how helpful is it to use financial ratios in setting goals for future performance? They can certainly be devised. But how easy is it to translate goals expressed in financial terms into strategies to achieve them?

Let us look more closely at the role of strategic management in an enterprise (Figure 9.1). We can see that, at a superficial level, strategic management is about converting an idea or vision into a commitment – one in which the owners or shareholders are prepared to invest. We need to examine it in more detail to see how it influences the performance of the processes 'above ground' – the processes which financial ratios are designed to measure.

117

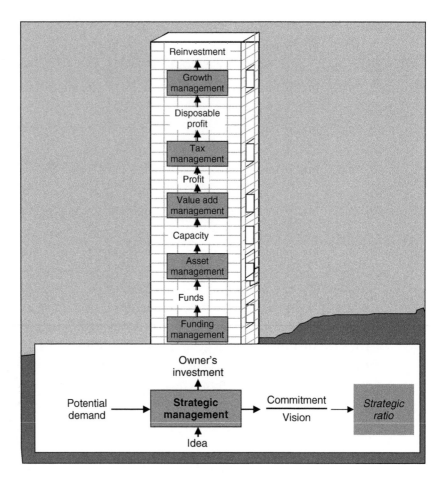

Figure 9.1 The strategic management ratio

The foundations of strategic management

As we delve into the foundations of a firm's strategy the steps involved in developing such a strategy can be mapped in more detail. Each of these smaller steps is critical to ensuring a sound strategy – one that supports the structure of the building. If a firm omits any of these, the whole fabric of the building may be unsafe.

The steps are not only relevant when an enterprise is being built. They also serve as a useful checklist when revisiting the vision of an enterprise, to ensure that it continues to be strong and versatile in response to change.

The process of strategic management is inevitably iterative and some steps will assume greater importance at some times than at others.

But there is a profound logic in the sequence of these steps and so we will start at the deepest and earliest level of the process of strategic management and work our way up through five steps in all before reaching the surface (Figure 9.2).

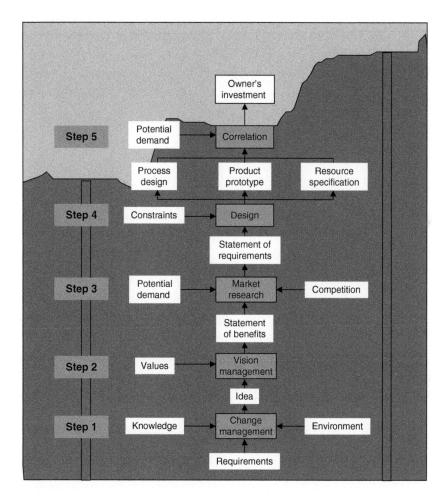

Figure 9.2 Five steps in the strategic management process

Change management

The origin of any enterprise lies in an idea or vision. But where do ideas come from in the first place; and how do they develop? At the deepest level of the foundations of an enterprise we find that change is invariably the catalyst for such ideas (Step 1). The need for change within a business can be triggered by one or more types of change happening elsewhere.

Changes may occur in the environment or in our knowledge of it, through scientific discovery. Or changes may arise in the requirements of individuals or other businesses as a result of corresponding influences upon them.

Such inputs to the *change management* process can trigger the need for a new response to requirements and thereby give rise to a new enterprise or organisation. Or it can raise the need to adapt existing ideas, whether in terms of the actual product or service they represent or the way in which they are produced and delivered.

Vision management

Whether an idea is new or has been adopted – and adapted – for some time, it is advisable to check the values that are inherent in it (Step 2). These values can influence whether and how it is accepted by all those contributing to its fulfilment: from those who 'own' it as shareholders and directors to those who 'buy into' it as employees, customers and suppliers.

These values not only relate to the way we conduct business, but are also inherent in the product or service itself. As a result of this process of *vision management* a 'statement of benefits' (and any risks or prohibitions arising from questionable values) can be drawn up. These benefits can then be weighed up to assess the genuine 'value' of the proposition and whether it is acceptable to those responsible for the enterprise.

Market research

Provided the potential benefits of the idea are acceptable and worth pursuing, the next stage of strategic management is to carry out *market research* (Step 3). This is to establish the exact nature and volume of potential demand. This research should include a study of existing ways in which requirements are being met, in other words the nature and size of potential or actual competition.

The purpose of such research should be to produce a clear 'statement of requirements' that the product or service seeks to meet. This can then form the basis for the design of a product or service that seeks to meet those requirements.

Design

If there is sufficient evidence to show that the idea, or adaptation, being considered meets the requirements identified in a way that is not currently being met, and if there are significant benefits to be shared, the next step is to proceed to *design* (Step 4).

Design should incorporate three strands: design of the process by which this idea will be realised; a specification of the resources required in the process; and a prototype of the product or service itself. It is during the detailed design work – if not before – that constraints will be identified. These may be technical, financial, legal or some other form. It is important to identify such constraints – whatever they are – before the owner starts to make a commitment of resources.

Correlation

The final step in the process of strategic management is to draw together the three strands of process design, product prototype and resource specification through a process of assessment or *correlation* (Step 5). This is to ensure that these three elements are compatible with one another and combine to meet the need as originally intended. By going through this final stage of the process, management can assess most effectively the nature and strength of potential demand and thereby evaluate the case for investment 'above ground'.

Such an evaluation should result in the equivalent of an 'artist's impression' of the intended structure above ground. It should include a financial plan of the investment and infrastructure required for it, and of the anticipated revenue and profit arising from it. As the structure is mapped out, the anticipated performance of each process can be expressed in the form of the financial ratios we have studied earlier.

The place of financial ratios in strategy

In this way the strategic management process can produce a financial plan, but how can we measure the effectiveness of the process itself? If we are to apply the same principle in using ratios to measure the relationship between inputs and outputs to a process, financial ratios are not appropriate – financial resources are not yet committed.

If we take each step in the process in turn we will need other ways to assess how effectively ideas are being created or adapted in the light of change. These steps cover respectively:

◆ the quality of values inherent in those ideas and their attendant benefits;
◆ how well potential demand is assessed and requirements specified;
◆ how well constraints are anticipated in design;
◆ how harmoniously the design components are correlated; and
◆ how fit for use the intended product and processes prove to be.

Financial ratios are not an appropriate tool for measuring each step in the strategic management process within the foundations. However, they can be useful in assessing the impact each step has on the operational processes above the ground. Again, we shall examine the foundations, step by step, to see how the performance of the edifice, as measured in financial terms, can be influenced by each one.

The influence of strategy on financial ratios

At the deepest level of strategy, *change management*, the ability of an enterprise to recognise and respond to change (Step 1) is critical to its success. A change in customer requirements has an immediate effect on the nature and level of value it is able to add. This may directly affect the profit margin and, if changes need to be made in an asset, this may affect the asset turnover ratio. Advances in technical knowledge and changes in environmental requirements can have a direct impact on asset management and the asset turnover ratio, and the latter can, in special cases, change liabilities to tax and thereby the effective tax rate.

The values which a business expresses, and how those values are established and developed, can have a significant influence on the relationships between the various stakeholders in the business. The motivation, conduct and loyalty of employees – often expressed under the heading of 'morale' – is very much influenced by how strongly they respect, identify with and find pride in the values of the enterprise. This can influence productivity and quality of service, thereby affecting the asset turnover ratio and profit margin.

The brand value of a firm's product or service is strongly tied up with the values it represents and this affects customer loyalty and thereby the revenue and profit margin which the firm can achieve. The synergy capable with suppliers is also determined by how compatible the values of firms in the supply chain are. This again can affect how a company structures its asset base and shares value add with its suppliers.

How a company stands by its values will influence how shareholders and investors view the level of corporate risk. This in turn will affect the gearing ratio and the opportunity for reinvesting profits in the business (the retention ratio).

Finally, how a company discharges its responsibility for tax liabilities and how it treats the environment has a wide impact on its reputation in the community.

While *vision management* (Step 2) deals with the intangibles of values and purpose, *market research* (Step 3) seeks to convert these into specific requirements. By enabling a firm to clearly differentiate its product and identify its target market, it can seek to achieve market share and profit margin objectives. However, market research need not be limited to the consumer market. In exploring the needs of shareholders and investors, a company can better understand their requirements on its gearing ratio and payout ratio.

Avoiding funding constraints will be one purpose of the *design* process (Step 4) within strategic management, and a financial plan is a key element. It should also uncover any technical, legal or ethical constraints which could impact its asset management or tax management strategies and thereby its asset turnover ratio and effective tax rate.

Finally, the process of *correlation* (Step 5), bringing the process, product and resource plans together, enables the balance within the 'building' to be assessed. Two companies may achieve the same return on assets with widely different mixes of profit margin and asset turnover ratios. This will be influenced by the nature of the product, the market, and each firm's asset base. But as conditions and requirements change, so it is important for a firm to review how its asset management and value add management processes work together.

Similarly a company's return on equity or dividend yield can be achieved in a number of different ways. These could reflect diverse combinations of component ratios that produce the same result in aggregate. It is important that management review these in the light of the level and mix of risk and reward they present for the various stakeholders in the business and monitor how they change over time.

Raising strategic questions

We stated earlier that the process of strategic management is inevitably iterative. In an environment where change is normal, the strategy for the enterprise needs to be constantly reviewed to ensure that the vision is still valid where circumstances, requirements or knowledge may have changed. And, if not, the vision may need to be adapted, modified or, if necessary, let go and replaced by another.

The Enterprise Stewardship Model provides a useful framework for such strategic reviews. By stepping through the model, management can raise strategic questions which get to the heart of the enterprise and its long-term value and success. Figure 9.3 gives examples of the kind of questions to address in order to test and appraise the strength of the foundations of the business.

The foundations

The best place to start the review is at the deepest level of strategy: the conditions that gave rise to the idea or vision for the enterprise in the first place (Step 1). Changes in circumstances, knowledge and requirements can occur very gradually and be almost imperceptible in the short term. However, provided the review is periodic and rigorous, it can identify even the most subtle of changes which can have a significant impact in the long term. Management then need to identify the appropriate response which utilises its unique resources and position in the market.

At the next level in the foundations, vision management (Step 2), changes in the essence of the idea should be checked as to any changes in values that arise. This may be the opportunity to confirm or enhance such values and to assess the benefits of doing so for the various groups of stakeholders. For instance, does the change give more or less authority to employees? Does it affect the environmental interests of the community? Does it enhance the experience of customers in purchasing or consuming the company's goods or

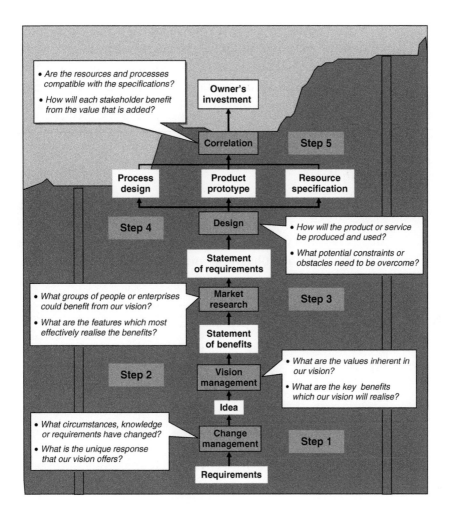

Figure 9.3 Checking the foundations

services? And does it meet the ethical needs of shareholders or their risk profiles for investment?

Changes in requirements or demographic profiles of customers can affect the particular groups that a business may be appealing to. As part of the firm's market research (Step 3) it should check from time to time the scope of the market it is appealing to and what other groups the changes enable it to appeal to in future. Given changes in technology, infrastructure and so on it is also important to reassess the most effective ways of realising those benefits so that the list of requirements is updated with changing features or priorities.

Changes in product and service specifications will inevitably call for design changes (Step 4). It is important to monitor how a product or service is being used and what potential obstacles or constraints need to be overcome. Finally, process design goes hand-in-hand with product and service design (Step 5). It may call for changes in resources required to carry out those processes in the most efficient and cost effective manner while not compromising the inherent value of those products or services.

The building itself

A similar exercise can then be applied to the edifice above ground. Figure 9.4 gives examples of the kinds of questions to address in order to ensure the respective floors of the building are robust and fulfil the investment below ground (Level A).

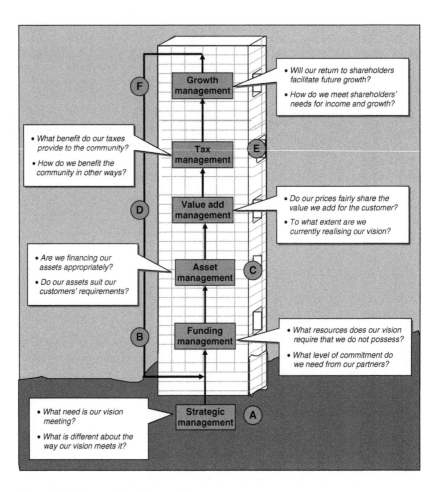

Figure 9.4 Strategic building maintenance

The review of resource requirements and specifications at Step 5 will inevitably lead to a reappraisal of funding requirements (Level B). It should incorporate a review of the level of risk and commitment required from different groups of financing partners: shareholders and lenders under various terms so that they are each satisfied with their balance of risk and reward.

Financial requirements may also arise from the nature of the assets under management (Level C) and it is important, as well as ensuring that assets continue to meet (changing) customer requirements, to assess whether the firm is financing its assets appropriately.

The process of managing the way value is added (Level D) is at the heart of the enterprise. A key strategic question is therefore to what extent such added value is being maximised and how it is being shared with the customer.

It is easy to lose sight of the benefit that a company provides through the taxes it pays. Taxes are invariably seen as a reduction in value rather than a transfer of it to the community. While a company may legitimately seek to minimise that transfer through tax management (Level E), it can nevertheless be refreshing to represent such transfer in terms of the infrastructure it provides for its own benefit and that of its stakeholders.

Finally, strategic questions need to be asked as to what growth the enterprise can sustain in realising its full potential (Level F). Managers should recognise and seek to meet the needs of both the enterprise, for sustainability and growth, and of its investors, for income and capital growth from their investment.

Each enterprise will have its own strategic questions to address in order to achieve long-term value and success. By using a holistic and comprehensive model it can ensure that such questions cover the full scope of the enterprise and, by an iterative process of asking them, can ensure that they produce consistent and sustainable responses.

Making the strategic connection: creating value and success

There is clearly a big step between setting a strategy and seeing results – between digging the foundations and measuring the financial dimensions of the building itself. We have looked at the place of financial ratios in strategy and the influence of strategy on financial ratios. It may have become clear that there is almost a leap of faith required to get from one to the other. So how can the gap be bridged?

The pictorial form of our model offers a clue. The planning and strategy that goes into the foundations is realised in the fabric of the building – the purpose and method by which the floors are put together and how each floor is organised. Financial ratios seek to measure the relationships between what is put into – and what is got out of – each floor. But, as we have seen, they can be crude attempts at this and do not necessarily explain what has caused the results or offer any guidance as to what to do to improve them.

And so we need something that translates strategy into results and explains those results in terms of the performance of activities we can relate to and do something about. As outcomes, financial results can be rather sterile and we need tools we can use to effect change so that we can maximise value and success, whether measured in financial terms or less tangible ones.

We therefore need to look inside the building as to how it is set out and what the dynamics are that produce the financial results that we are measuring. The building, or enterprise, is made up of a series of floors, or processes – six major ones at the level we have constructed. Imagine each floor containing a number of discrete areas, or sub-processes, and imagine these being made up of zones, or activities. In order to understand the connection between strategy and results we need a series of measures at each stage so that we can manage the outcome of our strategy and plans.

These measures are often described as *key performance indicators* (KPIs) and can take various forms. The closer they are to explaining the results the more likely they will need to be quantitative and objective, such as productivity measures. And the closer they are to strategy the more likely they will need to be qualitative, even subjective, such as the effectiveness of communication. In some respects they can provide the missing link between commitment and results in much the same way as activity-based costing provides the link and bridges the gulf between resources and products.

A *balanced scorecard* is an example of introducing this sequence or set of measures to reflect wider criteria for value and success than financial ones. While one of the four elements of a balanced scorecard is a 'financial perspective' the other three comprise a 'customer perspective', an 'internal perspective' and an 'innovation and learning perspective'.

A close examination of KPI's is beyond the scope of this book. But they provide a crucial link between strategy and results. The perspectives described within a balanced scorecard extend beyond financial measures but we will examine different perspectives on financial results themselves in the next chapter.

Responding to key challenges

1. The main steps within the strategic management process are
   - Change management
   - Vision management
   - Market research
   - Design
   - Correlation
2. The different steps within the strategic management process affect operational processes in different ways.
3. Key performance indicators can form the link between strategy and performance measured by financial ratios.

Conclusion

We have examined the process of strategic management and found financial ratios alone inadequate for measuring how effectively it is carried out. The quality of strategic management is to be assessed by how effectively an enterprise converts its vision into commitment. These are intangible factors to which it is difficult to apply a financial expression. However, we have seen that each step in the process can have a significant effect on the performance and sustainable success of the enterprise which financial ratios do seek to measure. And key performance indicators can serve to bridge the gap between strategy and results measured in financial terms.

How to maximise value and success

1. Relate strategic decisions to their direct and indirect impacts on financial ratios and performance in both the short and long term.
2. Consider efficacy and effectiveness as well as efficiency when making strategic decisions.
3. Use key performance indicators to bridge the gap between strategy and financial results.

10

Perspectives on financial ratios

> **Key challenges**
>
> 1. Who are the key stakeholders in a business?
> 2. What do they look for in a business?
> 3. How do they each view the financial performance of a business?

Introduction

In the Introduction to this book we set out to explain what financial ratios are seeking to measure and how to use them to maximise value and success for the business in which we are engaged. In mapping where financial ratios fit in we have studied the internal workings of a business and seen which processes they measure.

We have considered how financial ratios try to measure the efficiency, effectiveness or efficacy of an enterprise. We have also seen how they connect with one another through those processes and, in Chapter 9, how they are affected by a firm's strategy. But nowhere have we written a prescription for success or even described what success would look like for any one business.

So who determines what the criteria for success are, and who decides who is to benefit? This is the subject we shall address in this chapter. First of all we must consider who the key players are in a business, what their respective claims and contributions are, and what position they hold in our model of success.

The stakeholder groups

Perhaps the first people one should think of in a business are the *customers*. After all, if 'the customer is king' and they do not consider the firm has succeeded in meeting their requirements, or even expectations, they will not come back and there can be no future for the company.

As we saw in Chapter 5, an enterprise and its customers are invariably part of a supply, or 'value', chain. Just as a customer may not be the ultimate 'consumer', so the firm itself represents a customer to its suppliers. Therefore, in as much as a company sees itself as having a contribution to make in the success of its customers, so it should recognise the stake that *suppliers* have in its own success.

In a sense, all the stakeholders in an enterprise are supplying a critical ingredient to it – and thereby laying claim to benefits in return. Customers provide the original purpose for its creation as well as the ongoing income required for its sustenance.

In the conventional use of the term, 'suppliers' provide one element of 'supplies' in the supply chain. Other groups also supply key resources. Employees provide skills and effort; banks and capital markets supply funds; central and local government, as representatives of the community, provide an environment and infrastructure in which to operate; and any of these groups, among others, can be the source of ideas and vision for the future.

The distinction between suppliers and employees is also becoming less clear in some cases. Outsourcing and the use of short-term contracts has become a popular way of converting one to the other. However, in supplying skills and effort and being the ultimate custodians of knowledge in a company, *employees* hold a special position in the management of assets and creation of value in an enterprise.

A company operates within an economic and social infrastructure, and the provision of services in the local and wider economy can seriously affect the efficiency and effectiveness with which it operates. Those responsible for providing these services – the *community* in its widest sense – are therefore recognised as a stakeholder group in their own right, even though they may represent a disparate group of organisations and interest groups.

This group is sometimes portrayed as representing 'the environment'. But this is only one of the responsibilities for stewardship assumed by central and local government. And they are only two of the institutions that form part of this group.

The final group who make up the conventional list of stakeholders are the *shareholders* who supply the capital and have ultimate legal responsibility for a company. One might argue that one should start with this group, just as our model illustrates that it is the shareholders who are the first to raise their heads above ground with the initial investment in an enterprise.

There are other ways of classifying these groups of stakeholders and, as we have indicated, the distinction between them is not always clear. However there is one other group which we need to identify in order to encompass all the various contributions and claims of stakeholders. This group is characterised by the supply of ideas and vision to an enterprise. It is made up of those who created the original idea and those who take it on, adapting it as necessary towards its fulfilment.

We shall call this broad group the *entrepreneurs*. Their members do not need to be restricted to the board of directors, trustees or even senior management. They may be drawn from any or all of the other groups, and their role is crucial in leading an enterprise through all its plans and operations so that it achieves success in the way and shape intended.

We shall now explore the roles of each of these groups within our model and assess the contribution – and claim – that each has to the performance and success of an enterprise. In doing so, we will map their roles against the processes within our model and in the context of the financial ratios which are used to measure them.

The customer-supplier perspective and the profit margin

As we saw in Chapter 5, the supply chain can be mapped through the heart of an enterprise, its process for adding value (Figure 10.1). Customers have the role of realising the value being offered and return a share of that value through the pricing mechanism. They therefore have a perspective on what is a fair – and sustainable – share for themselves and the company. Suppliers contribute to the source of value add and will seek to share that equitably with the company. The profit margin achieved by the company thereby represents the company's share of value added by all parties.

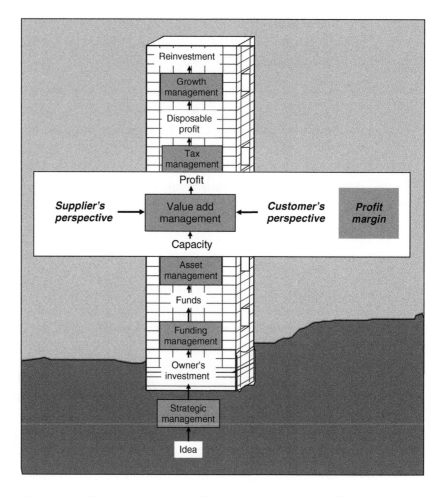

Figure 10.1 The customer and supplier perspectives on the profit margin

The employee's perspective and the return on assets ratio

As we have said, the employee is a unique form of supplier – one whose relationship with the enterprise is probably most personal and profound. It is a well-known (and somewhat tarnished) axiom that 'our employees are our greatest asset'. However, although they may not appear on the balance sheet they do invariably represent the most important asset in a company – more so as the value of a company is dependent on the knowledge or intellectual capital (IC) contained within it. It is therefore appropriate to link the role of employees to the process of asset management as well as value add management (Figure 10.2).

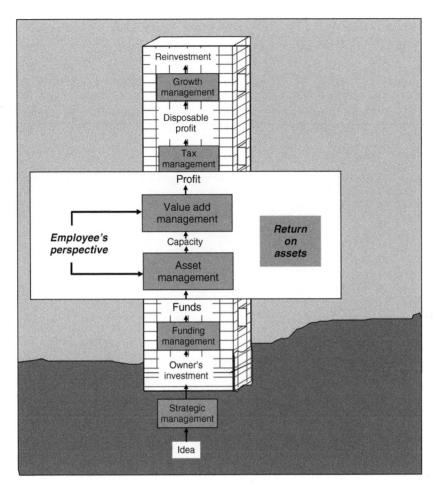

Figure 10.2 The employee perspective on ROA

The contribution from employees will be a key determinant of a company's asset turnover ratio and the quality of their contribution will have a direct impact on the profit margin. They therefore have a major role to play in the return on assets ratio that encompasses these two processes.

From their point of view, employees will also have a key interest in how the company manages its assets. This includes not only themselves directly, through training and other personnel policies, but also those assets that enable them to do their jobs effectively, develop their own potential and add to the quality of their lives generally.

The community perspective and the after-tax return on assets ratio

We have defined 'community' in its widest sense to include all those interests that contribute to the environment and infrastructure in which a company operates. There are therefore two processes within our model which will attract the greatest interest of the outside world (Figure 10.3).

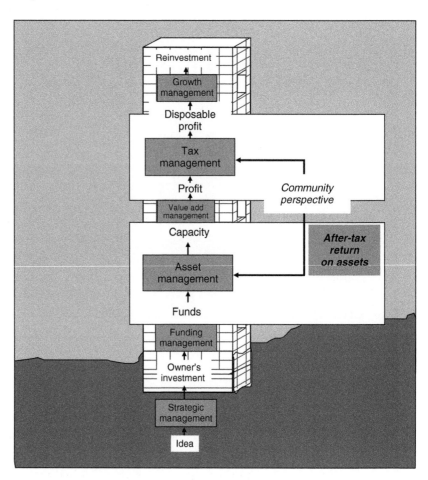

Figure 10.3 The community perspective on after-tax ROA

The first, asset management, involves the way the company affects the environment through its policies and practices. These extend from the use and treatment of scarce resources, including any pollution caused, to the application of equal opportunities and treatment of the disadvantaged in society. Asset management is therefore a key focus for the community perspective.

The other key interest of the community, as represented by the government, is the contribution the company makes to its tax management process. While it is in society's interests that companies make profits in order to share them with the wider community, it is also important for the reputation and standing of a company that it is seen to act fairly and legally in respect to its taxation policy and practice.

By focusing on a company's asset and tax management activities, the community perspective thereby spans those processes. The ratio of after-tax return on assets provides a composite measure of these processes and the community perspective can therefore present a counter-weight to the view taken by shareholders.

The shareholder and entrepreneur perspectives and the yield ratios

As we have seen, the interest of shareholders goes beyond return on equity, depending on the share of profits they wish to see distributed as dividends through the payout ratio. We have also discussed the range of interests that shareholders take in a company: from original owner to share-holder to investor. Certainly the shareholder, of all the stakeholder groups considered so far, has the broadest range of interest in a company, as illustrated in our model (Figure 10.4). The dividend yield – and its reciprocal, the reinvestment rate – embrace all the processes that lie 'above the ground', from funding management to growth management.

But the definition of shareholders as investors or even as legal owners does not give them the full status of the original owner or entrepreneur in creating the business in the first place and ensuring its future success. This role is often identified with the directors or trustees of a company or enterprise. And indeed they have a legal obligation to the company as a whole and not just the shareholders. But, to the extent that enterprises depend upon all groups of stakeholders for their continued efficiency, effectiveness and efficacy, members of any or all of these groups can make a strategic contribution to leadership.

Thus, although we have found it difficult to wrap a financial measure around the strategic management of a company, it is important that its foundations are not neglected in pursuit of 'superficial' measures

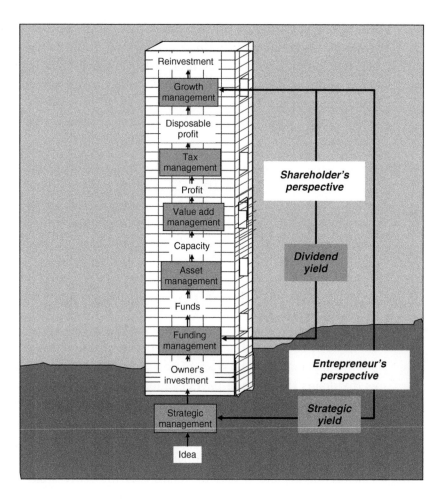

Figure 10.4 The shareholder and entrepreneur perspectives on yields

of financial performance above ground. For in the long run it is the components of that strategic management process which will define and determine the true success of the enterprise – its *strategic yield* (see Figure 10.4).

The leadership perspective on roles and relationships

The stewardship of an enterprise requires both management and leadership. Statutory requirements have become more extensive and detailed in an attempt to create rules for corporate governance. As a result, the obligations for compliance become more complex and onerous.

At the same time, the real value generated by enterprises is often based on relationships and loyalty rather than physical assets and transactions. Thus the complex set of relationships between a company and its stakeholders, as illustrated in Figure 10.5, is more like a community than a process. It has the features of an organism rather than an organisation.

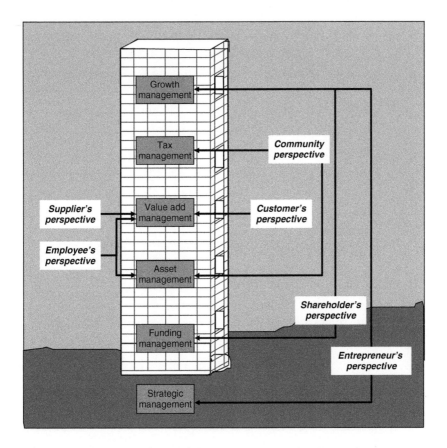

Figure 10.5 The leadership perspective on roles and relationships

Ratios can be valuable tools in measuring the performance of a business and its key processes. Money is, in a sense, the lifeblood of a business. It needs to be circulating and in good supply in order to maintain a healthy corporate body.

Financial ratios are therefore invaluable in measuring the efficiency and effectiveness of that blood supply. They can give warning of impending blood loss in order to avoid bankruptcy and death. They can indicate the quality of the blood supply through the value that the enterprise is adding and sharing with others. And they provide a universal language for measurement and comparison with other bodies.

However, sustainable success depends also on maintaining relationships with all those with a stake in a company. Only by maintaining relationships can each continue to benefit and make their contribution to the efficacy of the enterprise. Ratios are a useful tool for measuring the tangible. Financial ratios are a crude attempt at measuring value. But they are limited in their ability to measure relationships. Just as no enterprise will survive if it neglects any one of the key processes in our model – the building will collapse – so any one of the stakeholder groups has the power, if not the authority, to 'pull the plug' and withhold a company's licence to operate.

It is the role of leadership within an enterprise to keep alive and relevant the vision and values which sustain it. The success of the enterprise and the criteria upon which it is judged will ultimately go beyond the crude measures that financial ratios can offer and depend on the perspectives of the stakeholders who judge it.

Responding to key challenges

1. The key stakeholders in a business are its customers, suppliers, employees, shareholders and its community.
2. They each have different stakes and interests in a business.
3. They each have a different perspective on a business and its performance.

How to maximise value and success

1. Recognise the contribution of all stakeholders to the value and success of a business and the benefits that each group receives from it.
2. Encourage all stakeholders to recognise their interdependence in maximising the value and success available to them all.
3. Encourage all stakeholders to be entrepreneurs in maximising the potential value and success of a business.

Appendices

Appendix 1 The purpose of ratios: The three Eff's

Throughout this book we have referred to three dimensions of measurement in business: efficiency, effectiveness and efficacy. These dimensions are now defined in more detail. Table A1.1 provides some defining and relevant questions which can be applied to a business and are based on the structure of processes within the Enterprise Stewardship Model. Table A1.2 provides some examples of ratio measurements for each process and again relates them to each of the three dimensions of measurement.

Table A1.1 The Three Eff's – Definitions

Process	Efficiency	Effectiveness	Efficacy
	the economic use of scarce resources	*the production of a result or effect*	*the production of the results intended*
	Quantitative	*Qualitative*	*Quintessential*
Funding mgt	What is the cheapest way I can raise the funds I need?	What are the most secure and lowest-risk sources of funds?	What sources of funding will best help me to support and sustain the vision of the company?
Asset mgt	What are the least resources I need to produce what is required?	What is the best those resources can produce?	How can I best use those resources to develop them and enable our vision to be realised?
Value add mgt	How can I deliver my product or service at the lowest cost?	How can I maximise the value that people receive?	How can I optimise the benefit that our vision has the potential to provide?
Tax mgt	How can I minimise the amount of tax I pay?	How can I maximise the amount of profit available to the company?	How can I ensure that the tax the company pays complements our vision?
Growth mgt	How can I make best use of the distribution and reinvestment of profits?	How can I maximise the growth and value of the company from the profit available?	How can I achieve the greatest progress towards realising our vision from the profit available?

Table A1.2 The Three Eff's – Examples

Process	Efficiency	Effectiveness	Efficacy
	economic use of scarce resources	*production of a result or effect*	*production of the results intended*
Funding mgt	Average Interest Rate	Debt Coverage Ratio	Debt to Equity Ratio; Share T/O Rate
Asset mgt	Productivity Rates	Asset Turnover Rates	Employee Turnover; Asset Replacement Rates
Value add mgt	Gross Margin	Net Margin	Customer Loyalty
Tax mgt	Effective Tax Rate	NAT Profit Rate	Investment Equivalent of Tax Paid
Growth mgt	Dividend Payout Ratio	Cost of Capital Ratio; Book to Market Value Ratio	Actual to Plan Performance (Key Indicators)

Appendix 2 The source and application of financial data for ratio analysis

Throughout this book we have tried to use the language of activities and processes rather than bookkeeping and accounting to explain the use – and limitations – of financial ratios. There are other books which can explain the intricacies – and pitfalls – of calculating the ratios from any given set of accounts (see Further Reading). But that is not the purpose of this book.

It is our contention that a sound understanding of the principles will protect the analyst from such pitfalls. Despite (or in some cases because of) statutory requirements and the regulations of accountancy bodies, there is great diversity in the way that accounts are presented – what detail is included and what terms are used to describe it. It is therefore important for those wishing to analyse performance on the basis of financial accounts to be able to extract the correct information required or, if it is not readily available, to ask the right questions in order to obtain it.

As an aid in using appropriate financial data to calculate the required ratios, we therefore offer a 'route map' between the financial statements of an enterprise and the financial ratios as illustrated throughout this book in the Enterprise Stewardship Model.

The ultimate source of all financial data for analysis is the financial statements of an enterprise – its profit and loss account and balance sheet. To avoid unnecessary detail, we show the relevant elements of each in Figure A2.1.

The key financial ratios which we have covered require the following data from the profit and loss account:

◆ revenue
◆ net profit before tax
◆ net profit after tax
◆ dividends.

And the following data from the balance sheet:

◆ equity
◆ total liabilities
◆ total assets (divided for clarity into fixed and current).

These elements can now be related to the components of the respective financial ratios illustrated in our model (Figure. A2.2). Three (revenue, before-tax profit and after-tax profit) are used twice and, although total assets and total liabilities appear only once each, they

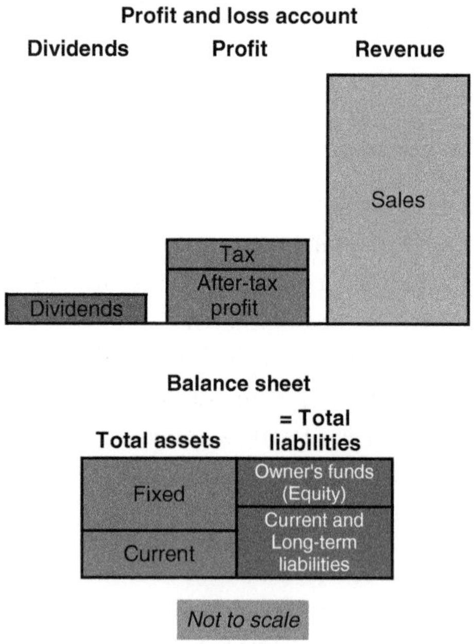

Profit and loss account
Dividends
Profit
Revenue
Sales
Tax
After-tax profit
Dividends
Balance sheet
Total assets
= Total liabilities
Fixed
Current
Owner's funds (Equity)
Current and Long-term liabilities
Not to scale

Figure A2.1 The source of financial data for ratio analysis

Reinvestment
Growth mgt
Disposable profit
Tax mgt
Profit
Value add mgt
Capacity
Asset mgt
Funds
Funding mgt
Owner's investment
Strategic mgt
Idea
Payout ratio
Effective tax rate
Profit margin
Asset T/O rate
Gearing ratio
Dividend yield
Dividends / NAT profit
×
NAT profit / NBT profit
×
NBT profit / Revenue
×
Revenue / Total assets
×
Total liabilities / Equity
=
Dividends / Equity
Profit and loss account
Dividends
Profit
Revenue
Sales
Tax
After-tax profit
Dividends
Balance sheet
Total assets = Total liabilities
Total assets
Owner's funds (equity)
Other liabilities
Not to scale

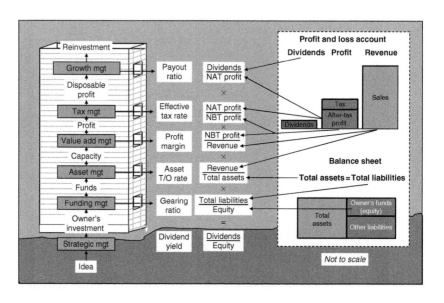

Figure A2.2 The application of financial data for ratio analysis

are the same values and therefore cancel out in the same way when acting as denominator and numerator respectively.

Worked examples

We have described above the generic process for obtaining data for ratio analysis. However, despite statutory requirements determined by Companies House (in the UK), companies still have leeway to present their financial statements in a variety of ways – and do so. It is therefore important to identify, within a company's financial statements, the key 'stepping stones' identified in our model in order to define the scope of each step in the business process. There now follows two worked examples of extracting data from original sets of financial statements and using the model to calculate and map the key ratios for those particular companies.

Figure. A2.3a shows the profit and loss account and balance sheet for a jewellery group in the conventional vertical form shown in the company's accounts alongside the diagrammatic representation of its key components. It provides all the elements required to complete our model of key financial ratios for the company and the first step is to identify these specific elements that we wish to extract. They have been highlighted in the statements and their position shown in the diagram alongside them.

Figure A2.3b shows these elements transferred to their respective places in the Enterprise Stewardship Model where the respective key ratios can be calculated and shown.

Figures A2.4a and A2.4b show the equivalent steps for an international oil company. In this case the labels attached to the financial statements are different but the essential process is the same.

(a)

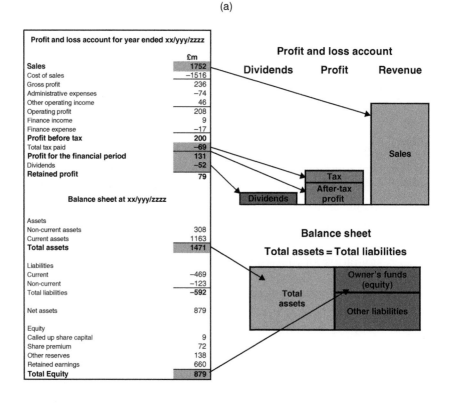

(b)

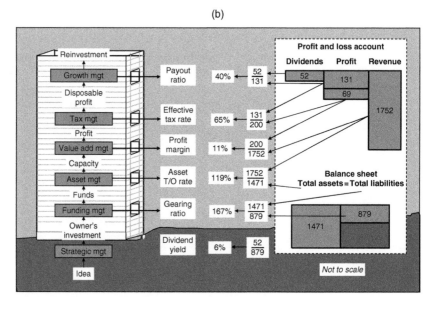

Figure A2.3 Worked example: A jewellery group

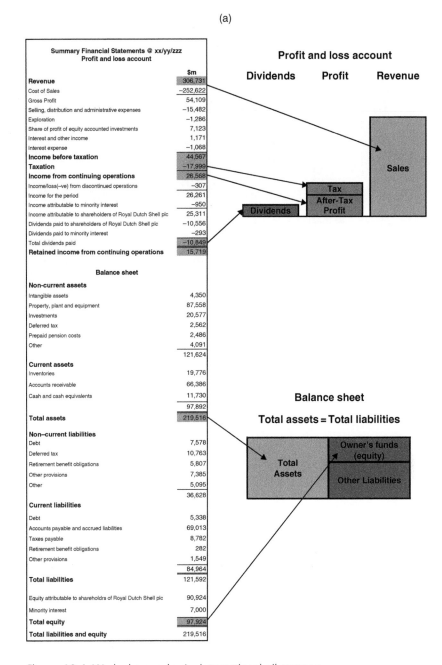

Summary Financial Statements @ xx/yy/zzz Profit and loss account	
	$m
Revenue	306,731
Cost of Sales	−252,622
Gross Profit	54,109
Selling, distribution and administrative expenses	−15,482
Exploration	−1,286
Share of profit of equity accounted investments	7,123
Interest and other income	1,171
Interest expense	−1,068
Income before taxation	44,567
Taxation	−17,999
Income from continuing operations	26,568
Income/loss(−ve) from discontinued operations	−307
Income for the period	26,261
Income attributable to minority interest	−950
Income attributable to shareholders of Royal Dutch Shell plc	25,311
Dividends paid to shareholders of Royal Dutch Shell plc	−10,556
Dividends paid to minority interest	−293
Total dividends paid	−10,849
Retained income from continuing operations	15,719
Balance sheet	
Non-current assets	
Intangible assets	4,350
Property, plant and equipment	87,558
Investments	20,577
Deferred tax	2,562
Prepaid pension costs	2,486
Other	4,091
	121,624
Current assets	
Inventories	19,776
Accounts receivable	66,386
Cash and cash equivalents	11,730
	97,892
Total assets	219,516
Non−current liabilities	
Debt	7,578
Deferred tax	10,763
Retirement benefit obligations	5,807
Other provisions	7,385
Other	5,095
	36,628
Current liabilities	
Debt	5,338
Accounts payable and accrued liabilities	69,013
Taxes payable	8,782
Retirement benefit obligations	282
Other provisions	1,549
	84,964
Total liabilities	121,592
Equity attributable to shareholdrs of Royal Dutch Shell plc	90,924
Minority interest	7,000
Total equity	97,924
Total liabilities and equity	219,516

Profit and loss account

Dividends   Profit   Revenue

Sales

Tax

After-Tax Profit

Dividends

Balance sheet

Total assets = Total liabilities

Total Assets

Owner's funds (equity)

Other Liabilities

Figure A2.4 Worked example: An international oil company

(b)

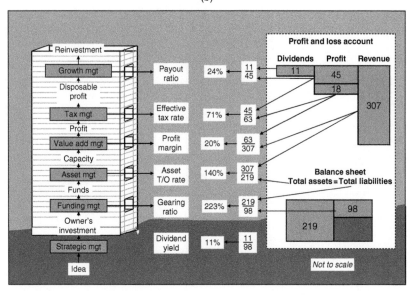

Figure A2.4 Continued

Appendix 3
A benchmarking example

	Company A £ m	Company B £ m
Balance Sheet		
Equity	**100**	**200**
Total Assets		
(= Total Liabilities)	300	800
Profit & Loss Account		
Revenue	1,200	2,400
NBT Profit	60	180
Tax	15	45
NAT Profit	45	135
Dividends	**15**	**40**
Composite Ratios	**(%)**	**(%)**
Dividend Yield	15	20
Return on Equity	45	67.5
Return on Assets	20	22.5

Figure A3.1 Benchmarking example – selected company data

In the above example company B is achieving a 20 per cent 'bottom line' dividend yield – something that may be attractive to potential investors who are looking for income from their investment compared to the 15 per cent currently being achieved by company A. However, such a summary measurement begs a number of questions and these can be addressed and explored by examining this ratio in detail, both in its component parts (results benchmarking) and the processes by which these are achieved (process benchmarking) together with their accompanying risks and implications. To illustrate this we will analyse each company's results and processes step by step, using the composite ratios described in Chapter 8 to 'unpeel the onion skin' gradually from the outside in. Figure A3.2 maps this analysis against The Enterprise Stewardship Model.

Despite producing a higher dividend yield, company B has a slightly lower payout ratio: 30 per cent compared to 33 per cent for company A. Thus company B is not only giving investors a higher level of income for their investment but is also retaining a higher proportion of its profit for reinvestment which should in turn enhance their capital growth. The reason it is able to do this is that company B's return on equity is significantly higher than A's (67.5 per cent compared to 45 per cent).

The next layers of skin to peel back are the effective tax rate and gearing ratio. In this example both companies are achieving the same rate of 75 per cent profit retained after tax – in other words achieving the same effective tax rate of 25 per cent. This might suggest

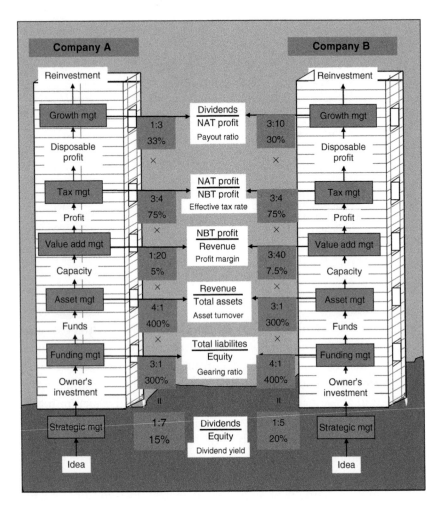

Figure A3.2 Benchmark mapping

they have similar infrastructures and processes for tax management. However, closer examination of their asset profiles and geographic investment may reveal differences at a more detailed level.

Company B is more highly 'geared' than A, with equity making up a quarter of its total liabilities compared to nearly a third in the case of company A. Company B's debt:equity ratio is 3:1 compared to 2:1 for company A. Company B's funding management therefore results in higher risks and rewards for their shareholders, perhaps justifying a higher return at this time given the risks of this being lower if market circumstances deteriorated for both companies alike.

Removing the layers of payout and gearing ratios focuses on the return on assets ratio which lies at the heart of the business. Here, company B's advantage in relative performance is reduced to a ratio of 22.5 per cent compared to A's 20 per cent, The gearing ratio has clearly been the single most dominant factor in contributing to its higher dividend yield and, now that this has been stripped out, the operating performance of the two companies appear closer in line with one another.

However, the similar performance of asset turnover ratios masks a significant difference in asset and value add management performances. Company B operates with a lower asset turnover but higher margin. Indeed the higher margin compensates for a lower turnover to produce a higher overall return on assets. This might result from a strategy of stocking higher margin products or being located in premium sites enabling higher prices. Their assets may be newer and therefore less 'written down' by depreciation, again enabling premium pricing. Closer examination would help to reveal any fundamental difference in strategy, branding or operational efficiencies between the two companies which would help to explain the different profiles in performance.

This is a simple and cursory example of comparing the results of two companies to identify underlying differences in process and thereby suggest opportunities to improve performance in the light of their attendant risks and impact on the company's vision for its product and/or service. This exercise can be helpful when looking at the industry in which one operates or to consider the options in achieving performance targets which may entail changing levels of efficiency and effectiveness to achieve them. However, unless the enterprise is driven purely by results, the efficacy of carrying out business in certain ways is a consideration before taking action purely on financial criteria.

Appendix 4 Further reading

This book has set out to explain the purpose of financial ratios, how they relate to the operation of an enterprise, and the value and pitfalls of using them as measures of performance in your business.

I have set out to equip the reader with an understanding of the principles involved in order that they can apply them to the specific circumstances of their business and their market.

It was not intended to provide a comprehensive list of all financial ratios that could be calculated or details of the calculations themselves. Neither does it try to compare ratios achieved by different companies in different industries or make an assessment of what is acceptable or exemplary.

A number of weighty tomes have been written and compiled over the years on the subject of financial ratios. However, the following books, available at the time of publication, complement this text by exploring certain aspects in more depth.

1. *To see how data is extracted from an example company's financial statements and used to calculate its key management ratios*:

Walsh, Ciaran (2005). *Key Management Ratios.* Prentice Hall. Illustrates the ratios that act as 'guiding stars' of operating performance, corporate liquidity, determinants of corporate value and management decision-making.

2. *For a comprehensive and thorough list of every ratio, formula and statistical analysis available*:

Bragg, Steven M. (2006). *Business Ratios and Formulas: A Comprehensive Guide.* John Wiley & Sons. A comprehensive list of nearly two hundred ratios and operational criteria for measuring business, categorised under thirteen measurement categories.

3. *To collect data on financial ratios in different industries*:

Troy, Leo (2006). *Almanac of Business and Industrial Financial Ratios.* Prentice Hall. A thorough and detailed encyclopedia of statistics drawn from company accounts and reported by industrial sector.

4. *For a comprehensive and thorough definition of terms*:

CIMA Publishing (2005). *CIMA Official Terminology.* Elsevier. A useful glossary of financial and technical terms endorsed by the Chartered Institute of Management Accountants.

5. *Below is a list of a further ten books published on the subject over the last thirty years*:

Bhattacharya, Hrishikes (1995). *Total Management by Ratios*. Sage.

Dun & Bradstreet (1998). *Key Business Ratios: 1994*, 12th revised edn. Dun & Bradstreet.

Ketz, J. Edward, Doogar, Rajib K. and Jensen David E. (1990). *A Cross-industry Analysis of Financial Ratios*. Quorum Books.

Neely, Andy (1998). *Measuring Business Performance*. Economist Books.

Ramsden, Philip (1998). *The Essentials of Management Ratios*. Gower.

Temple, Peter (2001). *Magic Numbers*. John Wiley & Sons.

Tyran, Michael (1992). *The Vest Pocket Guide to Business Ratios*. Prentice Hall.

Vause, Bob (1999). *Guide to Analysing Companies*. Economist Books.

Viscione, Jerry A. (1983). *Analyzing Ratios: A Perceptive Approach*. National Association of Credit Managers.

Westwick, C.A. (1987). *How to Use Management Ratios*. 2nd edn. Gower.

Index

Accounting principles or
    'concepts', 83–4
Accruals concept, 83
Acid test ratio, 40
Activity-based costing, 67–8
Asset management, 8–10
    assessment of real value of asset
        turnover ratios, 57–9
    component ratios in, 50–1
    current asset turnover
        ratios, 51–7
    in financial terms, 48
    tangible assets, 48–50
Asset turnover ratios, 23
    see also Asset management

Balance sheet, 22–3
Balanced scorecard, 128–9
Benchmarking, a business, 104–6,
    159–61
Brand value, 65
Build-to-order principles, 52

Capital allowances, 82
Cash flows methods, 93–4
Cash turnover ratio, 53
Collection period, 52
Company strategies, 63
Composite ratios, 26–8, 30, 103–12
Cost management, 66–8
Current asset turnover ratios
    cash turnover ratio, 53
    debtor turnover ratio, 52–3
    inventory turnover ratio, 51–2
    working capital turnover
        ratio, 53–4
Current assets, 39
Current ratio, 40
Customer loyalty, 65, 74
Customer relationship
    management (CRM), 74
Customer-supplier perspective,
    on profit margin, 135–6

Debtor days, 52
Debtor turnover ratio, 52–3
Depreciation, 55–6, 71, 161
Disposable profit, 25

Dividend cover, 42
Dividend yield ratio, 30, 109–10
    shareholder and entrepreneur
        perspectives, 139–40
Dividends, 91–2, 110
Dividends per share (DPS), 110

Earnings per share (EPS), 110
Effective tax rates, 24–5
    see also Tax management
Enterprise Stewardship Model
    (ESM), of business process,
    xvi–xvii
Enterprise value chain, 73
'enterprise zones' and taxes, 82
Equity captial, 22
Evasion and fraud, risks of, 84

Fixed assets, 39
Fixed asset turnover ratio, 54
    intangible fixed assets, 56–7
    tangible fixed assets, 55–6
Funding management, 6–8
    amount of funds required,
        38–9
    borrowing of funds, 41
    costs of funding, 43–4
    forms of ownership, 41–3
    principle of matching, 39–40
    sources, 40

Gearing ratios, 21–2
    see also Funding management
'Going concern' principle, 66, 83,
    91, 94, 110
Growth management, 13–15
    application of disposable
        profit, 89–90
    case for growth, 92
    cash flows, 93–4
    company's perspective, 92
    dividends, 91–2
    options for growth, 95–6
    profit flows, 94
    shareholders perspective, 91
    sources of growth, 96
    value flows, 94–5

Illiquidity, 39
Intangible fixed assets, 56–7
Internal rate of return, 94
Inventory turnover ratio, 51–2
Investment appraisal
    techniques, 93–5

Key performance indicators
    (KPIs), 128

Leadership perspective, on roles
    and relationships, 140–2
Leasehold purchasing, 41

Market differentiation, 63
Market-led strategy, 63
Market research, 120
Matching principle, 39–40
Measuring value, with financial
    ratios, xi
  asset turnover ratios, 23
  composite ratios, 26–8, 30
  dividend yield, 30
  effective tax rates, 24–5
  gearing ratios, 21–2
  payout ratio, 25–6
  profit margin, 24
  return on assets ratio, 28–9
  return on equity ratio,
    29–30
  strategic ratios, 21

Net after tax (NAT) profit, 25,
    29, 89
Net before tax (NBT) profit, 25,
    29, 81
Net present value, 93

Overtrading, 40
Ownership, forms of, 41–3

Payback method, 93
PAYE, 79
Payout ratio, 25–6, 89
Pricing element, of value add
    management, 70–2
Productivity, measure of, xi
Profit and loss account, 23

Profit management
  activity-based model, 69–70
  resource-based approach, 69
  value based approach, 69–70
Profit margin ratio, 24
  customer-supplier
    perspective, 135–6
Profits, 80–2, 110
  rules for charging against, 82–3

Ratio, defined, xi
Resource-based costing, 67–8
Resource-based strategy, 63
Retention ratio, 26, 88–90
Return on assets ratio, 28–9, 106
  community perspective, 138–9
  employee's perspective, 136–7
Return on equity ratio, 29–30,
    106–8

Small- and medium-size
    enterprises, 83
'Special development areas' and
    taxes, 82
Stakeholder groups, 133–5
'Straight-line' method, of
    depreciating assets, 82
Strategic management, 5–6
  balanced scorecard, 128–9
  foundations, 118–21
  influence on financial
    ratios, 122–4
  key performance indicators
    (KPIs), 128
  review of strategic steps, 124–7
  role of financial ratios in, 121–2
Strategic ratios, 21

Tangible assets, 48–50
Tangible fixed assets, 55–6
Tax management, 11–12
  accounting principles or
    'concepts', 83–4
  process and administration, 80
  risks of evasion and fraud, 84
  rules for charging against
    profits, 82–3
  types of profits, 80–2

Taxes Acts, 82
Three eff's', xiv–xv, 75, 117, 147–8

Units of measure, xi

Value add management, 10–11
  cost management, 66–8
  pricing element of, 70–2
  profit management, 68–70
  profit margin ratio, 64–5
  relationship between profit and
    value added, 65–6
  value chain concept, 72–4
Value added tax (VAT), 79
Value and success, meaning,
  xiii–xiv

Value chain concept, 72–4
Value creation, process of
  asset management, 8–10
  funding management, 6–8
  growth management, 13–15
  strategic management, 5–6
  tax management, 11–12
  value add management,
    10–11

Working capital turnover
  ratio, 53–4

Yield ratios *see* Dividend yield
  ratio

Please note that the previous printing included a CD-ROM attached to the inside back cover of the book.

The material is now only available on the companion website:

http://www.elsevierdirect.com/companion.jsp?ISBN=9780750684538

CPI Antony Rowe

Chippenham, UK

2017-03-31 21:07